MEETING COMMON CORE TECHNOLOGY STANDARDS

Strategies for Grades 6-8

Valerie Morrison | Stephanie Novak | Tim Vanderwerff

International Society for Technology in Education
EUGENE, OREGON • ARLINGTON, VA

Meeting Common Core Technology Standards
Strategies for Grades 6-8
Valerie Morrison, Stephanie Novak, and Tim Vanderwerff

Editor: Paul Wurster
Associate Editor: Emily Reed
Production Manager: Christine Longmuir
Copy Editors: Jennifer Weaver-Neist, Kristin Landon
Cover Design: Brianne Beigh
Book Design and Production: Jeff Puda

Library of Congress Cataloging-in-Publication Data

Names: Morrison, Valerie, author. | Novak, Stephanie (Stephanie M.), author. | Vanderwerff, Tim, author.

Title: Meeting common core technology standards : strategies for grades 6-8 / Valerie Morrison, Stephanie Novak, Tim Vanderwerff.

Description: First edition. | Eugene, Oregon : International Society for Technology in Education, [2016] | Includes bibliographical references and index.

Identifiers: LCCN 2016001275 (print) | LCCN 2016006326 (ebook) | ISBN 9781564843708 (paperback) | ISBN 9781564845689 (Mobi) | ISBN 9781564845696 (ePub) | ISBN 9781564845702 (PDF)

Subjects: LCSH: Middle school education–United States–Computer-assisted instruction. | Educational technology–Study and teaching (Middle school) | Common Core State Standards (Education) | BISAC: EDUCATION / Teaching Methods & Materials / General. | EDUCATION / Computers & Technology.

Classification: LCC LB1028.5 .M63775 2016 (print) | LCC LB1028.5 (ebook) | DDC 371.33–dc23

LC record available at http://lccn.loc.gov/2016001275

First Edition
ISBN: 978-1-56484-370-8
Ebook version available

Printed in the United States of America

ISTE® is a registered trademark of the International Society for Technology in Education.

About ISTE

The International Society for Technology in Education (ISTE) is the premier non-profit organization serving educators and education leaders committed to empowering connected learners in a connected world. ISTE serves more than 100,000 education stakeholders throughout the world.

ISTE's innovative offerings include the ISTE Conference & Expo, one of the biggest, most comprehensive ed tech events in the world—as well as the widely adopted ISTE Standards for learning, teaching and leading in the digital age and a robust suite of professional learning resources, including webinars, online courses, consulting services for schools and districts, books, and peer-reviewed journals and publications. Visit iste.org to learn more.

Contents

About the Authors

VALERIE MORRISON graduated with an elementary education degree from Northern Illinois University (NIU) and began her career as a classroom teacher. She became interested in teaching with technology early on and was a computer teacher for two years at a K-8 private school. Morrison then switched to the public school system, where she obtained a master's degree in instructional technology with an emphasis in media literacy from NIU. She gained 14 years of experience as a technology director / technology integration specialist and technology coach. Morrison worked closely with teachers and students to plan and differentiate lessons and projects that integrate technology. She taught technology workshops and classes for teachers and oversaw the technology program at her school. (She loves working with kids, teachers, and technology!) Like her coauthor Tim Vanderwerff, Morrison regularly served on her district's technology committee, and was involved with integrating current state and district standards with the latest educational technologies. She presented at various conferences, including a presentation in Springfield, Illinois, to state legislators, where she and coauthor Stephanie Novak briefed legislators on how schools use technology. Morrison has recently switched career paths and is now teaching education classes at the college level; she enjoys using technology to teach the next generation of teachers. She also has time to write now, which allows her to further educate the current generation of teachers.

 **STEPHANIE NOVAK** knew from a very young age that teaching and working with kids was the right career path for her. She graduated from Northern Illinois University with a master's degree in reading and earned a reading specialist certificate from National Louis University. Novak started teaching at the middle school level but eventually settled in the elementary school system. As a classroom teacher for 27 years and an extended-learning teacher and coach for the past seven years, she has always felt learning should be fun and meaningful. Novak was on her school district's technology committee for many years and regularly tried new technology in her classroom. As an instructional coach, she encouraged teachers to help students grow in their learning at a pace that allows for the most intellectual and personal growth. For the past two years, Novak guided Grade 1–5 teachers through the Common Core State Standards, teaching them how to blend these standards with rigorous curriculum and prepare students for the digital age. After many years in education, Novak recently retired. She now looks forward to applying her years of experience in a consulting capacity for administrators, teachers, and students. She also plans to continue to publish stories that describe her successful experiences in the field of education.

 **TIM VANDERWERFF** has an extensive background in teaching and technology that began in the '70s. Although writing this book was a new experience, trying out new experiences in education are second nature to him. After graduating from Illinois State University and then earning a master's in educational administration from Northern Illinois University, Vanderwerff saw many federal and state initiatives come and go in his 33 years of teaching. Starting as a classroom teacher in grades 2–5, he was on his school district's technology committee for many years and regularly tried new technology in his class during that time. Vanderwerff eventually moved to the library media center at his elementary school in 1987. He was the librarian and the technology teacher, and he provided tech support for the building for many years. In 2010, he was asked to be a teaching coach, which involved sitting in on grade-level team meetings, finding resources for the new Common Core State Standards, supporting individual teachers and teams in the classroom (both with technology and with the newest educational strategies), and advising new teachers. Vanderwerff is recently retired, allowing him to devote more time to writing about the field in which he is so passionate.

DEDICATIONS

For my husband, Glenn, whose constant support helps me to follow my dreams.
   —Valerie Morrison

To Bill; all my family; my confidant, Kim; and my District 96 friends.
   —Stephanie Novak

To my family: Kim, Eric, Michael and Kristina.
   —Tim Vanderwerff

Acknowledgments

We are grateful for the contributions of our friends, teammates, colleagues, and assistants with whom we worked throughout the years and who helped us come up with ideas for our first four books–this series. Working with so many talented people, we appreciate the collaboration and teamwork that allowed us to learn a great deal about coaching and technology. We would especially like to thank Val Kieser and Bridgette Calamari for their contributions to the practical ideas chapters in this book (Grades 6–8).

We would also like to thank our families for all of their amazing support during the writing of this series. During the many times we spent meeting, editing, and struggling to write, their unwavering support was truly appreciated.

Also, we would like to thank the editors and their staff at ISTE for their insight, guidance, and patience. Their ongoing support has been much appreciated as we've gotten familiar with the process of publishing.

Introduction

Have you ever found yourself sitting in a meeting wondering, "How am I ever going to change all my lessons to fit the new Common Core State Standards?" At that moment, you also realize your district wants you to integrate the latest digital-age technology, and that has you asking yourself, "Where will I get this technology? Will it be provided for me, or am I responsible for purchasing and providing the technology?"

All of this might seem overwhelming—what is a teacher to do? First, you might turn to your teammates and colleagues for help and support. Perhaps your district provides current technology development for staff on a regular basis and has instructional coaches to help teachers chart this new territory, planning new lessons, bringing in resources, and infusing technology. In reality, most districts don't have all of this support. Yet teachers are especially in need of technology when considering their clientele: students.

Until recently, every state was doing their own thing when it came to standards. The Common Core State Standards (CCSS) is a U.S. education initiative seeking to bring diverse state curricula into alignment with each other by following the principles of standards-based education reform. The CCSS is sponsored by the National Governors Association Center for Best Practices (NGA Center) and the Council of Chief

State School Officers (CCSSO), and a vast majority of the 50 U.S. states are members of the initiative. So, if you are in a Common Core state, there are big changes happening. Even if you're in a state that's not adopting Common Core, there is a high likelihood your curriculum will soon look very similar to the CCSS initiative.

We, as coaches, have an important role in helping you, the teachers, and your students during this transition. Our hope is that you are in a district that provides high-quality professional learning experiences regularly to help teachers understand the shift from existing state standards to the CCSS. Professional development, along with this book and its resources, will help you identify the changes you will need to make to guide your instruction using CCSS with technology and support you in transferring new knowledge and skills to the classroom. It is a large task, but focusing on specific goals for student learning utilizing the CCSS with technology will have a positive effect on student achievement. And this will improve your teaching.

CCSS were designed to prepare K–12 students for college and career success in the areas of English language arts, math, science, and social studies. CCSS defines the knowledge and skills students should have in their K–12 education, with an emphasis on learning goals as well as end-of-year expectations.

Most states have had English language arts and math standards in place for a few years. However, these standards vary, not only in coverage but also in levels of rigor. CCSS is very explicit about what is expected of students at each grade level. Students, parents, teachers, and school administrators can now work together toward common goals. CCSS will be consistent from school to school among states choosing to adopt the standards. If students or teachers transfer to different schools, they will all be assured that learning expectations will be the same. Any student, no matter where they live within a Common Core state, can be assured that they will be able to graduate from high school, get ready for college, and have a successful career.

The standards first launched in June 2009. State leaders from the CCSSO and NGA developed them together with parents, teachers, school administrators, and experts from across the country. Both national and international research and evidence informed development of the standards. After public comment, organizers released the final version of the CCSS in June 2010.

The CCSS were written in a clear, understandable, and consistent manner to align with college and work expectations. These standards contain rigorous content, as well as an application of knowledge through higher-order skills. CCSS are evidence based, and they build on the strengths and lessons of current state standards.

Writers of CCSS also gathered information and advice from top-performing countries to ensure that U.S. students are prepared to succeed in a global economy and society. Here is a helpful link from the Common Core State Standards Initiative's **"About the Standards"** page: **http://tinyurl.com/26f7amp**.

Transition to the Common Core will be a challenging task for your students as well as for you. With the implementation of these new standards, students will be expected to become self-directed and critical readers, writers, and thinkers. At the same time, you will need to make adjustments. In fact, you will need to shift your entire instructional practice.

Shifting your instructional practice will require a great deal of work and commitment, but this will all be well worth the effort for both you and your students. By breaking things down into small steps, the transition will seem less overwhelming.

This book is part of a collection of four books designed to help teachers connect technology to the Common Core in their classrooms. We learned how to do this by teaching together, and we have more than 85 years of combined teaching experience. As teammates, we worked with students, teachers, and administrators to integrate technology in the same school district. Our hope is that you will think of this book as your coach, because we can't be with you personally. We hope to show you how to integrate the newly embedded tech-related language found within the standards into your everyday curriculum.

In Chapter 1, we address some of the issues that your students face and discuss how important it is to tailor their learning experiences. Today's students are the first generation to truly grow up in the age of the internet, complete with emailing, texting, instant messaging, social networking, tweeting, and blogging. Teaching this new generation of children, teenagers, and young adults can be challenging because of how digital technology has affected their brains and behaviors. The Common Core curriculum has kept this new generation of students in mind, and so will we.

In Chapter 2, we explore the importance of engaging and educating parents. We follow this up with a discussion in Chapter 3 about the equipment you need to teach the standards, and we show you how to address the roadblocks that stand between you and this technology. There are always roadblocks that educators commonly face, and we hope to show you how to get around them effectively so that you—and your students—can succeed. We should also mention that although we are sharing many tools and resources with you, we are not affiliated with any company. The programs, apps, and websites listed in this book are simply those that we feel support the standards.

In Chapter 4, we discuss effective staff development, and we explain in Chapter 5 how the CCSS is organized. Chapter 6 takes a deeper look at the specific standards for the grade level you teach. With these standards in mind, we show you how to begin, offering several classroom-tested lesson ideas in Chapters 7–10 that will ensure your students are satisfying the tech-related benchmarks outlined in the CCSS.

We realize that technology is constantly changing and that digital tools come and go. To make certain that you continue to have the most current resources at your fingertips, visit **our website (http://tinyurl.com/oexfhcv)**. The website password for the 6-8 book is: MCC68TS. There, you will find an updated list of the apps, software, and websites mentioned in this book.

Let's begin by taking a closer look at today's generation of tech-savvy students and the skills they bring to the classroom.

Chapter 1

Today's Students

A two-year-old taking a selfie? Seven-year-olds tweeting? No doubt about it, today's students come to school knowing more technology than ever before. New educational research suggests that offering a variety of learning opportunities, including lots of technology options, may be the best way to engage today's generation of learners. Educators need to respond to this generation and address their unique learning needs. We, the authors, believe this so passionately that we think a chapter about this subject is a must in any book about teaching in the digital age. Technology must be made available to students. Technology must become ubiquitous.

The CCSS are designed to bring school systems into the new century. They are designed with the tech-savvy student in mind. Actually, the standards are designed with their future workplace in mind. That is the driving force behind the technology we see in the standards and why teaching to your students' future needs is extremely important. Please keep this mind as you read this chapter.

Who Are Your Students?

The students you now have in your classroom grew up using digital technology and mass media. According to Debra Szybinski, executive director at New York University's Faculty Resource Network (http://tinyurl.com/pqwr7va), this generation is:

> ...a generation characterized by some as self-absorbed, attention-deficit-disordered, digital addicts who disrespect authority and assume that they can control what, when, and how they learn, and by others as smart, self-assured, technology wizards, who follow the rules, and who are on their way to becoming the powerhouse generation. Clearly, this is a generation like no other, and that has posed an entirely new set of challenges both in and out of the classroom for faculty members and administrators alike.

Some of you are part of this younger generation. If so, you were the first to truly grow up in the age of the internet: emailing, texting, instant messaging, and social networking. Yet the current generation is ever changing. Those born even 15 years ago did not have technology so pervasive that it was with them 24/7. Many students entering school now are completely immersed in technology outside of school.

Ironically, at many schools, there is a disconnect to students' real lives and their way of learning. Schools are often islands of 20th-century thinking in a 21st-century world. Schools must do a better job of reaching the current generation of students; they need to respond to and address students' unique learning needs. Technology needs to be constantly available to students at school.

What Does This Generation Know and Do?

Many children entering kindergarten now have access to desktop computers, smartphones, tablets, and/or laptops at home. These children begin using all or most of these devices by the time they are three years old. Whether you go to playgroups, parks, or wherever, you're likely to see young children who are working on their parents' tablets or smartphones (or begging to use them!). These students come to us with skills that include (but are not limited to) swiping to work an app; navigating a mouse to play computer games; operating their own electronic devices, such as children's learning tablets, handheld learning devices, and interactive video games; and hunting and pecking on the keyboard to send emails. Also, our tech-savvy students can take videos and photos using a tablet or smartphone, as well as converse with someone by texting, blogging, and messaging. Most have been exposed to the internet and understand that they can find almost any kind of information that they are seeking.

Because they have so much information at the touch of a button and constant stimulation around them, this generation is often attempting to multitask. It makes sense to them to watch TV, send a text, and find out what the weather will be all at the same time!

Some say that the current generation has hovering parents and a sense of entitlement. While this may be taken as a negative, having parents who are involved with their children and their children's school is a good thing, as it strengthens the home–school connection. Students who have parents who are involved in their academic life can be better students, and they are less afraid to try new things. We, as educators, need to recognize these traits and use them to help students reach their maximum potential.

Being social is very important to the students in this tech-savvy generation. They are certainly the "in touch" generation, with immediate access to texts, emails, social networking sites, and even the sound of a human voice at the other end of the line. This generation is lost when their smartphone or tablet breaks down; they feel "cut off from the world" when they don't have instant access to the internet.

How Has Technology Affected Students' Minds?

By the time they're in their 20s, today's students will have spent thousands of hours surfing the internet and playing video games. This vast amount of screen time seems to be shortening their attention spans. At a time when their brains are particularly sensitive to outside influences, excessive screen time affects the way they learn and absorb information.

Furthermore, this generation does not read books to find information. Online search engines are prevalent in providing all of the information they need quickly, without having to go through a book from cover to cover. With access to an overabundance of information, they need to be skilled hunters who know how to sift through data quickly and efficiently. This new learner doesn't necessarily read from left to right or from beginning to end. Visuals help today's students absorb more information than they do from straight text. Thus, students become better scanners, a useful skill when confronted with masses of online information in a world that's full of noise and multiple stimulations. So, most modern students have learned to block out distractions while they focus on the task at hand.

How Has Technology Affected Behavior?

Because of the constant use of technology, there is less and less face-to-face communication taking place. We all have seen instances of parents and children sitting next to each other without speaking at a restaurant. Instead, they simply sit and quietly engage with their individual tablets or smartphones.

There are many debates about how technology helps or harms the development of a student's thinking. Of course, this depends on what specific technology is used, as well as how and with what frequency it is used in school. Our duty as educators is to decide what technology to use in the classroom and when, because technology influences students' thought processes. We educators need be aware of this effect to guide our students in becoming 21st-century learners.

How Do We Move Beyond the ABCs?

Education has gone through a monumental transformation in the last 20 years. Some changes have greatly improved the way teachers educate, while others are still under evaluation. The great debate between play-based preschool versus learning-based preschool is a case in point. What we have found during our years as teachers is that to progress in the classroom, teachers have to adapt to the times, adopting new techniques while continuing to use time-tested methods. Success in teaching a new generation of students isn't based solely on what educators are teaching them but, rather, how educators are teaching them.

We have seen our share of success stories and our share of students who struggled for reasons that are completely preventable when these students have the right tools. For these highly activity-scheduled and gadget-oriented students, traditional one-size-fits-all teaching is no longer effective. Sitting behind a desk, listening to the teacher talk, and reading from a textbook are completely ineffective. This generation of students needs to be engaged in active and interactive learning to enhance their knowledge. They do not want technology just because it is "cool." They need technology because it drives their world now and will continue to drive their world in the future. They are looking for something dynamic to make learning come alive—to make it different and interesting every day. Being connected accomplishes that goal.

How Can Educators Succeed in the Digital Age?

Thinking that technology is a new toy that will go away or doesn't have a place in education is no longer an option. We educators need to embrace technology and tap into what our students are already coming to us with, using it to advance their learning. But this technology cannot just be digital worksheets!

This is not always easy, especially when students know more about how to use the technology than many teachers. Therefore, it is our duty to catch up and make sure we know what our students know. This can be done in many different ways; however, the easiest way is to do what they do: pick up tablets or smartphones and start playing with them! Once we have the background skills to know what our students know, we can then move forward. We simply need to remember that technology is a tool. And we can use these tools like anything else we use in education—manipulatives in math, novels in reading, and microscopes in science, just to name a few.

Of course, this new reality being imposed on and by the current generation has implications for you as a teacher. It used to be that students conducted research by using books that were from credible publishers, and those books went through rigorous editing and fact checking. This generation uses the internet almost exclusively. If your students get all of their information from the internet, then you must teach them media literacy skills. This skill set has become extremely important in an information age where children need to discern fiction from fact on the internet when, sometimes, we adults have trouble differentiating it for ourselves.

You need to tap into what your students are experiencing every day and use it to your advantage. Many of your current students will work in very social settings but in a different way than previous generations. Let them work often as partners or in groups to create multimedia presentations or digital videos. Because they love to send emails and video chat, let them email, instant message, or video chat with students around the world! This generation is good at multitasking. Allow them to do more things at once, such as opening multiple screens while taking notes on a research paper. Students all know how to use a smartphone, so when on a field trip, let them record a video of what they are seeing. They are used to constant noise and stimulation. Do not make them work quietly at their desks; rather, they should work with hands-on activities like live apps or green-screen technology. Students know at a very young age how to navigate the internet. Let them run to the computer when they have a question instead of asking you for the answer.

We know this new generation of children, teenagers, and young adults can be challenging because of how digital technology has changed their way of learning and behaviors. The following chapters will further address some of these issues and how learning needs to be specialized, giving more examples of how to integrate technology with the new CCSS. The Common Core curriculum has kept this new generation of students in mind, and so will we.

 **Chapter 2**

Parent Education

The past decade has been financially difficult for schools. States across the country have had to slash education budgets because of downturns in the economy. If your district's budget was not affected by financial cuts, it is among the few. As for the rest of us, we have had to achieve more with less. To make matters even more challenging, we now have new standards that ask schools to immerse students in technology—a very expensive task. Having parents on your side in this budget struggle can be very helpful.

In the years since the CCSS were written and adopted by most states, some attitudes toward the standards have changed. More recently, parents and community members have begun to question them. So it is important, as a teacher, to be proactive in getting the word out about what is going on in your classroom. Work with parents and the community to educate them about CCSS in your state, district, and school. Parents only want what is best for their children, and a little reassurance from you can go a long way.

This reassurance begins with listening to parents. Ask them about their concerns. Answering their questions with facts will help them to better understand why your state adopted the standards.

The following are just a few of the technology concerns that have been raised about the CCSS recently. Knowing about them and other controversial issues allows you to defuse concerns before they become major issues.

Why Do Parents Need to Know about Technology Standards?

You don't need technology to read and you don't need technology to do math—civilizations have been doing both for centuries. Nevertheless, you must admit that technology does help in both areas. If we were still at the turn of the last millennium (1000 AD), we would be hand-copying books. The printing press brought books to the commoner and education to those who wanted to learn. The abacus is fine but hardly as good as a calculator or a computer. Technology marches on so that we can advance, learn more, and pass that knowledge along to the next generation.

The computer revolution of the last century is finally hitting the classroom with the encouragement of the CCSS. Before these standards, the pervasive use of computers was for schools with money or those who could write winning grants. Even so, many schools that were thought to be advanced had not integrated technology into everyday learning. The Common Core is the first set of widely recognized standards to do that. But why do parents need to know about them? There are several reasons.

First, keeping students versed in the fundamentals of technology will enhance your teaching tremendously, and students' parents can help with this at home. Survey parents to see if they have internet access and broadband at home. What kind of equipment do they use—do they have cameras or video capabilities? What do they allow their children to use? Knowing what your students have or do not have at home evens the playing field in the classroom. Encourage parents to teach their children how to use tablets, computers, video cameras, and other mobile devices so their children come more prepared to school.

Second, learning doesn't just happen at school. You need to educate parents because they are the main support system for learning away from school. Consistent, clear standards now put forward by CCSS enable more effective learning. Knowing what technology and what software will be used to master these standards greatly assists parents and, in turn, their children. Look at the **Harvard Family Involvement Network of Educators (FINE, http://tinyurl.com/hguh777)** for the latest research and insights on how to get students' parents involved.

Third, technology can instantly link parents to what their children are learning. Knowing assignments, communicating with teachers, and understanding what is expected are all improved with today's technology. There is even an article out there (DeWitt, 2013) about a principal who tried "flipping" parent communication, which you might try too. Whatever you implement is a win-win for you and your students. Take advantage of technology in communication; don't shun it. It will make your life easier.

Finally, we are becoming a smaller, more codependent world. To have a world-class education that keeps our nation and civilization moving forward, all students need to be well versed in the newest technology. That is what the CCSS are all about! The Common Core State Standards Initiative's mission statement affirms, "The standards are designed to be robust and relevant to the real world, reflecting the knowledge and skills that our young people need for success in college and careers" (Council of Chief State School Officers & National Governors Association Center for Best Practices, 2010). In other words, the CCSS is designed for your students' success as adults in the work world, where technology is integral.

Even so, parents must be a part of this endeavor or their children will still struggle to succeed. Involving them is as important to you, as is any other aspect of your students' learning. Do not think of parent education in the CCSS as an add-on—a tool to be used if you have time. Investing in your students' parents and having them on your team benefits you and lessens your load. In a synthesis of studies done on families, communities, and schools, Henderson and Mapp (2002) stated, "Efforts to improve children's performance in school are much more effective if they encompass their families. Regardless of income level or education background, all families can—and often do—support their children's success." (p. 208)

What Issues Do Parents Have with Technology in CCSS?

Parents may ask you about some of the controversial things they are hearing in the news related to the Common Core. One controversy involves a misunderstanding about standards and curriculum. Standards describe what students should know; curriculum is how they get there. For example, even though there is no standard for cursive writing or keyboarding, that doesn't mean it won't be in your school's curriculum. Curriculum is still developed locally. Educate parents who are concerned that they have no control over their child's curriculum—they still have the ability to contribute to what is taught in their local school.

Another controversy centers on test scores from states that adopted the CCAA early on: scores decreased. Although it may or may not be true in your district, scores quite often decrease when the format of the tests changes. One example is when students go from paper-and-pencil tests to digital assessments. According to Swanson (2013), if your school changed tests, then a result might be decreased scores until students become familiar with the new format. The best way to combat this is to have other digital tests in the classroom throughout the year, to make your students feel more comfortable with the new format.

A common concern we have heard as teachers and as CCSS coaches is that the federal government will be able to collect the data of individual students because of these digital tests. This has been a particularly heightened apprehension recently. The fact is, there are laws passed by the U.S. Congress (2010) that prohibit the creation of a federal database with students' personally identifiable information. Although the law is in place, you should still be vigilant about keeping this sensitive data secure. You are the first line of defense and need to have procedures in place. Please go over your district's student privacy policy. If there is none, push hard to make one.

How Can Parents Help with Assessment Technology?

As the teacher, you should help parents and community members understand the types of questions and problems that students are asked to solve on the new digital assessments. During parent nights, open houses, and/or in newsletters, introduce parents to the **Partnership for Assessment of Readiness for College and Careers (PARCC, (www.parcconline.org)** and **Smarter Balanced Assessment Consortium (www.smarterbalanced.org)** websites. You can download sample questions to show to parents; and it can also be helpful to put new assessment questions next to old assessment questions so everyone can directly observe the shift.

If your state is going to use the Smarter Balanced test, have parents use the sample questions at the PARCC site to test their children at home. The sample Smarter Balanced test can also be used to prepare for the PARCC test. Both tests' questions are similar and based on the CCSS.

Don't forget the basics. Make sure parents know what kind of equipment the students will be tested on, and have them use similar equipment at home if possible. This will make the device a secondary concern so your students can focus on the test. And send home a sample question weekly so parents can become familiar with the changing assessments. Make sure some of the sample test questions you send home require students to use technology to answer the question, as this will be included on the assessments.

How Can Parents Help Students Meet Technology Standards?

Parents need to see the value of having technologies at home that can help their children achieve more. At the same time, home technology will help you accomplish these new curriculum tasks that, as we teachers know, are daunting, to say the least.

A recent poll by the Leading Education by Advancing Digital (LEAD) Commission (2012, p. 23) found that parents and teachers believe students who lack home access to the internet are at a significant disadvantage. Home access to broadband is viewed as important to learning and doing well in school for the following reasons.

- Home access greatly exceeds anything that your students could ever bring home in their backpacks.

- Home access allows parents to become more involved in their child's school-work and allows for more effective communication between parents and school, thus promoting greater student success.

- Having home access vastly expands the time your students can learn and explore.

- Home access leads to greater collaborative work, engaging students in online group homework homework. (This last point dovetails perfectly with many of the new CCSS technology initiatives).

Home access needs to have your active support. At the beginning of the year, run a workshop for parents about the kinds of technology you will be using and why. Teach them how to monitor their children for internet safety as well. You may want to call on your library media specialist or tech specialist to help you if they are available in your school.

Of course, you may teach in an area where parents do not have the funds to have broadband access or technology at home. Following are a few ways to address the issue.

- For homes that have broadband but no computers/tablets, start a program that allows students to check out resources from the school overnight.

- Have after-school clubs or homework help where technology is available.

- Open the school in the evenings for parents and students, providing them access to teachers and to the technology they need.

- Apply for one of many grants available from different levels of government, foundations, and companies to help with your school community's access to technology.

Wherever you teach, parent education is the key to student success with the state standards. Lack of information is one of the main reasons parents are opposed to the CCSS. Being a proactive partner with them will defuse most objections that arise—from parents and from others in the community—and actually create proponents of what is going on in your classroom through this challenging time. Having parents as partners can only help when you are faced with technology needs, such as lack of hardware and software, lack of assistance, and gaps in your students' tech knowledge.

Parent education is only part of the puzzle, however; you must first educate yourself about the CCSS and technology before you can effectively educate anyone. To address this, we have included a chapter on staff development (Chapter 4). But before we explore your professional development options, let's take a closer look at the roadblocks you may encounter on your journey to get technology into your classroom.

Chapter 3

Roadblocks to Technology

U nless your school or district has unlimited funding and gives you completely free reign on your purchases, you have hit roadblocks in your quest for classroom technology. Chances are that you do not have the student technology to become a fully stocked digital-age learning environment, but you are not alone. In this chapter, we provide ideas to best use and manage the equipment and software/ apps you do have, and we explore ways to get more. It is our hope that when we come to the later chapters on practical ways to integrate your technology into the new Common Core curriculum, you will be better prepared to maximize your resources.

What Are the Roadblocks to Accessibility?

If it is not possible to provide all of your students with tablets or laptops, providing half the class access to this technology is the next best thing. This allows you to work with small groups or pairs of students. Another option is to share technology with the classroom next door to gain at least some time with a full class set of laptops or tablets.

Lack of Funding for 10–12 Tablets/Laptops per Classroom

One option is to have each grade level share a cart of 15 laptops or tablets in addition to a roving cart that any classroom can access. We would suggest grade-level sharing of technology with no more than three sections, as more sections limit student use further. If there are four or more sections in a grade, more carts should be added. This will allow the grade level to have access to at least half a class set. When you need a full class set, use the mobile cart to fill in the gaps. Another way to share additional mobile devices is to divide the 15 laptops or tablets into sets of five for each of three classrooms and then have teachers share devices if a class needs more. You could also place all 15 laptops or tablets on a cart and provide a signup sheet for as-needed use.

Only 4–6 Laptops/Tablets per Classroom

You can have half the class double up on the tablets at one time or you can share with other classrooms near you to get more. To accomplish the latter, you have several options: you could pick a time every day when two or three classrooms share their laptops or tablets for an allotted amount of time; you could have certain days when you each have them; or you could ask for them informally. The key is easy accessibility.

Computer Lab Limitations

A computer lab with enough computers for all of your students is another great resource especially if it includes a tech or media center teacher or assistant. This is great because everything is in a set location and there is another knowledgeable teacher available to help. The negative is that you have to sign up for certain times, and everyone must work on the computers at the same time. If you have access to tables in the lab or in a nearby learning space, however, you have the opportunity to do other things with students who have finished their work on the computer, forming smaller work groups as you would in a traditional classroom.

1:1 Initiatives

Many districts are moving to a 1:1 tablet model for tablets or laptops, but if this is not the case in your district, then you will be more limited. More than likely, you will not have a full class set to yourself. If you are able to get a set to share, the easiest arrangement is to schedule times to use the devices. However, with such limited class time and many students per class, splitting up a class set so teachers get four to five devices per class may be a better option. It will just take more planning on your part to outline how your students will divide up their technology time.

At this level, enlisting students' smartphones is another option. Many students have them and bring them to school. Your district should discuss how to use these resources to their advantage while not interfering with the learning process. Some states are already using student-owned devices in their schools and have begun writing policies for them. About.com has a great article about addressing cell phone issues in schools— "Cell Phone Policy" (by Derrick Meador, http://tinyurl.com/ptb6eaz).

Additional Equipment

How do you choose additional technology to better equip your classroom when your budget is already tight or inadequate? Aside from laptops and tablets, it is imperative to have a multimedia projector so that all students can see lesson materials, projects, resources, and so on. Other equipment that is valuable includes:

- **Document cameras:** You will use these every day to display written books, worksheets, student work, and the like. Once you have one, you won't know how you got along without one!

- **Interactive whiteboards:** These are great for engaging students, especially during whole-group instruction.

We could have included interactive response systems as well; however, with so many new websites available that can turn your laptops, tablets, or smartphones into interactive technology, buying response systems is no longer necessary.

Some interactive websites that are free (and may offer an upgrade for an affordable fee) are:

- Socrative: (www.socrative.com)
- Exit Ticket: (http://exitticket.org)
- Annotate: (https://annotate.net)

Keeping Up with Students' State Assessments

Different groups developed PARCC and Smarter Balanced to test for college and career readiness starting from third grade onward. Your students may be tested three or four times a year. PARCC and Smarter Balanced (with very few exceptions) are the two main tests that states use to provide teachers the information they need to help students become successful with the Common Core standards. These two assessments are computerized and have certain technology requirements, but they allow traditional paper-and-pencil versions when necessary. (Teachers should still be aware that traditional versions may be phased out eventually.)

We will not address the specifics of network requirements; just know that your school or district will need to meet certain operating system and networking specifications whether they are using the Smarter Balanced or the PARCC assessment. Additionally, your network must be able to address security requirements to keep student information safe. Following are the informational sites to help you find what you will need.

- **Link to technical requirements for PARCC: (http://tinyurl.com/jmhyrey)**

- **Link to technical requirements for Smarter Balanced: (http://tinyurl.com/nuaqy6u)**

How Do We Overcome Software and Hardware Roadblocks?

You cannot benefit from technology if you don't have it. It is also difficult to share it if you don't have enough of it. You need it on time and easily accessible if you truly want to use it seamlessly. This may be the biggest roadblock. We discussed above how you can use different configurations of new or existing hardware in your school. The more pervasive the technology, the easier it will be for you to achieve the goals set forth by the Common Core.

Sources of Funding

If you don't have enough equipment and/or software, you can apply for grants. While there are more grants available for economically disadvantaged districts, some are accessible to all districts. State and federal grants are available, for example, especially if you can link your needs to the Common Core. The Bill & Melinda Gates Foundation and big companies like Google, Target, and Staples give to schools. Ask your PTA/PTO for money. Many districts have foundations that grant teachers money. You could even ask the PTA/PTO to do a fundraiser for new technology. Following is a list that is by no means complete but offers a great place to start.

GOVERNMENT

- **21st Century Community Learning Centers (http://tinyurl.com/7nx37vb):** This funding is designed to get parents and the community to actively support your work in the classroom.

- **Individuals with Disabilities Education Act (IDEA, (http://tinyurl.com/77b2dwa):** These funds are for students with disabilities.

- **Grants.gov (http://tinyurl.com/k8fybkt):** Search this site for all available federal grants. These grants include:

  - Investing in Innovation Fund (i3)

  - Race to the Top Fund: The government provides grants for Race to the Top specifically for the CCSS.

  - Title I, Part A–Improving Basic Programs Operated by Local Educational Agencies

  - Title I, Section 1003(g)–School Improvement Grants (SIG)

  - Title I–Supplemental Education Services (SES)

  - Title I, Part C–Migrant Education

  - Title I, Part D–Prevention and Intervention Programs for Children and Youth Who Are Neglected, Delinquent, or At Risk

  - Title II–Professional Development

  - Title II, Part D–Enhancing Education Through Technology (EETT)

  - Title III–English Language Acquisition State Grants

  - Title VII, Part A–Indian Education

- **Computers for Learning (http://computersforlearning.gov):** This government program encourages agencies to transfer their used computers and related peripheral equipment directly to schools.

- **State Government (http://tinyurl.com/oexfhcv):** Look for your state's educational website in this online index.

FOUNDATIONS

- **Bill & Melinda Gates Foundation (http://tinyurl.com/odwcrra):** This is the largest, private foundation in the world. Its primary aim in the U.S. is to expand educational opportunities and access to information technology.

- **The Foundation Center (http://foundationcenter.org):** This independent, non-profit, information clearinghouse collects information on foundations, corporate giving, and related subjects.

- **Foundations.org (http://tinyurl.com/7sf3c):** This online resource provides an A–Z directory of foundations and grant makers.

- **The NEA Foundation (http://tinyurl.com/or2qc56):** This teacher association gives grants in several areas.

COMPANIES

Many of the companies that manufacture the products we use every day have educational initiatives that offer grants for public schools. Following are just a few.

- **Target (http://tinyurl.com/cdt25kz):** Target offers grants in many areas, including: education, the arts, and public safety.

- **Toshiba (www.toshiba.com/taf/k5.jsp):** Toshiba also offers math and science grants for Grades K–5.

- **Google (http://tinyurl.com/pm9gar4):** Google has several sites dedicated to corporate giving. Google for Nonprofits is a good place to start your search.

- **Microsoft Corporate Citizenship (http://tinyurl.com/p62et7u):** These grants are available for after-school programs.

- **Staples Foundation (www.staplesfoundation.org):** Staples Foundation for Learning teaches, trains and inspires people from around the world by providing educational and job skill opportunities.

- **CenturyLink Clarke M. Williams Foundation's Teachers & Technology Program (http://tinyurl.com/otej8rl):** These grants are designed to help fund projects that advance student success through the innovative use of technology. Teachers in public or private PK–12 schools in CenturyLink's residential service areas are eligible to apply for a Teachers and Technology grant.

OTHER RESOURCES

- **National Charter School Resource Center (http://tinyurl.com/ph2ytng):** This resource website has many links to funding opportunities.

- **eSchool News (www.eschoolnews.com):** This is a great grant resource for K–12 and higher education.

- **Internet@Schools (http://tinyurl.com/nnh5n9d):** This online magazine for education provides a vast list of free resources, grants, and funding.

- **Scholastic (http://tinyurl.com/nd3t97t):** This educational mainstay has many great grant resources too.

Free Software and Apps

Software and app purchases are a challenging roadblock, especially if your district or school doesn't provide enough funding. Fortunately, there are many free resources. Search app stores and type in "free." Free sites, such as Google Docs, are also great places to start. In addition, there are entire sites with free services geared toward the CCSS.

If you are in a small district or a private school, or if you live in a state where funding is limited, follow the money. Go to websites in states and at schools that do have the funds. Look at websites in wealthier school districts near you. Do they have CCSS lessons, activities, and technology ideas that are free to anyone on the internet?

Many states have CCSS resources posted for free! Take advantage of them. For example, New York has many helpful suggestions at **engageNY.org (www.engageny. org/common-core-curriculum)**. Utah has also published a very resourceful Common Core site, which can be found at the **Utah Education Network (UEN, http://tinyurl. com/l2e532).**

Free software and apps are also available from private companies. These sites usually have ads, or they may want you to purchase add-ons; you and your district will have to judge their value for yourselves. More examples of free applications and websites will be given in the "Practical Ideas" chapters of this book.

What Other Roadblocks Must We Solve?

Systemic educational roadblocks can take many forms, which are often unintended or unavoidable. Here are three common challenges teachers face.

Misguided Policies

Some districts or schools require that all classrooms have the same apps or software. They don't allow teachers to choose what they prefer, and this can be frustrating. If your district wants all software to be the same, you might try explaining why each grade level and each teacher would benefit from using different software, apps, and equipment appropriate to their students' needs.

Some districts implement policies that do not allow teachers to use technology as a tool. Instead, they force teachers to use technology when other mediums or tools make more sense. For example, we discovered a district that required teachers to teach with a tablet 85% of their instructional time. This district even required students to bring tablets to gym class and physical education teachers to use tablets in every class period. School leaders who enforce this kind of policy know very little about infusing technology into the classroom. It would be better to achieve higher technology use through staff development and individual coaching (for example, through the use of this book) than by generating untenable policies that don't actually affect meaningful student learning.

To counter these policies, speak to your principal, go to a technology meeting, or attend a board meeting! Explain that technology is a tool and that the CCSS does not expect you to use technology every second of the day. There is a time and place for technology just as there is a time and place for math manipulatives, a calculator, a book, and even a pencil. Balance is the key. If anything is overused, it (and your effort) is set up for failure.

Parents

Parents will ask the question, "Why do we need new technology?" Have a discussion at PTA/PTO meetings, open house nights, and board meetings about what you will be doing or would like to do with technology. Explain that the CCSS expects everyone to integrate technology, and this is important for today's students. Please refer to the chapter on parent education (Chapter 2), which has specific suggestions about many of the issues that become parental roadblocks.

Staff Development

Teacher training is so important. You need to have professional development in the area of technology for yourself as well as for your students. If you have a technology coach, great! Spend a lot of time with this coach—set up weekly meetings. They can help you as well as model or co-teach with you. There are many professional development opportunities online as well as off-site in the area of technology. Refer to Chapter 4 to learn how to get staff development outside your district and how to best get around these roadblocks!

How Do You Get the Help You Need?

One of the key components of using technology is getting help. It is easier for middle school students to work independently with technology and follow directions. However, it may still be difficult to manage a class of students who are all trying to use technology at the same time. This is also the case when teachers try to work with a small group while the rest of the class is doing something else on tablets. Inevitably, something goes wrong with someone's computer, so many middle school districts use student technology assistants.

It is extremely helpful to have another set of hands. If you have assistants who come to you on a regular basis to help, this is a great resource. You can call on these assistants when you need them, which allows greater freedom to work with the whole class—assuming you have enough equipment.

If you do not have access to assistants, you might try using parent volunteers. The worst part of using volunteers is inconsistent attendance. However, if you can find a parent or two who is willing to come in on a regular basis, they can be a great help. You will need to find time to train your volunteers of course, but once you do, most will be savvy enough to pick up what they need to do in class.

Make sure that you post passwords where it is easy for students to find them. Forgotten passwords are an annoying occurrence, so having them easily accessible for all will help you manage the situation comfortably.

Another option is to work with your fellow teachers. Consider arranging your schedules so that you each take extra students while the other uses technology with a smaller group. Overseeing fewer students makes technology use much easier to manage.

Create peer groups that have a mix of tech-savvy students and those who struggle with technology. This is especially effective at the middle school level. Making the most of available technology is all in the management of it.

Although there can be many roadblocks that prohibit you from using classroom technology the way that you would like, there are ways to overcome these challenges. By using the suggestions given in this chapter, we hope you will overcome any roadblocks that lie in your way and that you have most everything you need at your fingertips.

Chapter 4

Staff Development

> When technology integration is at its best, a child or a teacher doesn't stop
> to think that he or she is using a technology tool—it is second nature. And
> students are often more actively engaged in projects when technology tools
> are a seamless part of the learning process.
>
> —"What Is Successful Technology Integration?" (Edutopia, 2007)

Without a doubt, today's student comes to school with a strong background and understanding of technology. This generation of tech-savvy students is interested, motivated, and even driven by technology. As you will see, CCSS has explicit technology standards within grade levels. But technology, as a tool, needs to be infused in all other CCSS standards as well. Having a tech-savvy classroom for today's students is the best way to create a 21st-century learning environment.

Truly integrated technology is ever present but invisible. You can use technology as a tool for instruction—as a way to vary the way you present information. You can also provide technology options for students as a way for them to engage in content skills. And students in your class should be given opportunities to create and share their new learning with a myriad of technology tools. The CCSS are not just about presenting information to students; today's students need to be able to plan, reason, analyze, evaluate, and create. Technology integration in today's classroom will do just that—it will not only allow your students to become more engaged in the learning process but empower them to gain a deeper understanding of their learning.

A plethora of articles have been written about the success of CCSS and how good professional development for teachers and staff is a significant key to its success. Technology plays a very valuable role in guiding and fostering this effective professional development, as well as helping to boost current professional-development resources and practices. And technologies that make tools available to teachers on an ongoing basis present a solid jumping-off point for successful classroom integration.

Research has found that sending teachers to workshop-based professional development alone is not very effective. Approximately, 90–100% of teachers participate in workshop-style or in-service training sessions during a school year and through the summer. While workshops can be informational and timely, teachers need opportunities to implement new teaching techniques, not just learn about them. Thus, professional development needs to be ongoing and meaningful to your own professional circumstances. The most effective professional development also uses peer coaches and mentors to implement new learning in class.

How Do You Create a Technology Plan?

You need lots of support and tools to utilize and sustain technology in your classroom. If you do not have a district or school technology director or coach, how do you develop a plan to get yourself (as well as your fellow colleagues) what is needed? You can be the pioneer to get the technology ball rolling.

Following are suggestions to help you begin the journey of infusing technology in your classroom. Although this should not be your task alone, sometimes it falls to a single individual to blaze the trail. Fortunately, there are many online resources that can assist you with creating a technology plan. **Edutopia** is a well-known place to start, offering (among other things) **"Ten Steps to Effective Technology Staff Development" (http://tinyurl.com/oesjsmn).**

The first step is to put together a technology committee with as many representatives from different buildings and grade levels as you can. It would be great to include administration staff as well as a district office representative. Parents, students, and outside technology experts can only enhance your committee.

Next, come up with some ways to show how you and your students can use technology in the classroom. Providing specific examples of students working with technology to address the ISTE Standards and the CCSS would be powerful!

Develop a detailed questionnaire for teachers to express their classroom needs, frustrations, and fears. This questionnaire can also serve as a place for teachers to describe what they hope to learn from professional development, including technology goals they would like students to pursue in class.

Ask students to describe the ideal state of technology in their classroom. Ask them how they envision the state of technology in their classroom in one year, two years, five years, and so on. Then place the ideas from this brainstorming session in a public document so everyone on the committee and in the community can see and refer to it.

Lastly, conduct a teacher survey using the **ISTE Standards for Teachers** as a guide **(www.iste.org/standards)**. These standards outline what teachers should know and be able to apply in order to teach effectively and grow professionally. ISTE has organized them into the following five categories:

1. Facilitate and inspire student learning and creativity

2. Design and develop digital-age learning experiences and assessments

3. Model digital-age work and learning

4. Promote and model digital citizenship and responsibility

5. Engage in professional growth and leadership

Each standard has four performance indicators that provide specific, measurable outcomes. You can use them to ascertain teachers' technology comfort level, attitude, and integration use in your school. Answers could be on a scale, such as "proficient enough to teach someone else," "able to hold my own," "a little knowledge," or "scared to death to even try." It may even be helpful to have teachers identify three to five areas that they feel are most important to improving technology within the year. Providing a space for them to write an explanation is also important, as they may not be able to rank themselves on a scale when they can't quantify what they don't know. Writing a paragraph about where they stand with technology might be easier for them. The data you gain from this survey should be shared with your building, other participating schools, the administration, and the district office. And you may want to consider repeating this comfort-level survey several times throughout the year.

Once you've determined the proficiency of staff members, you can enlist their help to create a digital folder of suggested lesson plans, activities, and projects for all to access and use. Your colleagues will not only be able to implement the folder's learning opportunities in their classrooms but add to the folder as they try new things. Something you may want to consider having is a reflection page to accompany any lesson, activity, or project posted. This will help others learn from and refine the ideas as they implement them on their own.

Additionally, your meetings, questionnaires, and survey results will identify teachers, staff members, parents, and administrators who have expertise in specific technology areas. Talk to your principal or district administrators to see if funding is available to pay for the planning time and workshops your experts may wish to lead. (As a rule of thumb, for every hour of professional-development class time, it takes at least two hours of planning.) Opportunities also need to be offered to your experts to advance their professional development. Perhaps you can even find a way to tap into the technology expertise of students, parents, and/or community members by having them lead some of your professional-development workshops. If possible, build in this professional- development/collaboration time at least once a week. Carrying on conversations about the workshops at team meetings, staff meetings, even lunch is a great way to foster and gain interest in what you and your committee are doing.

Even if you are not willing or able to head up a technology committee, there are many things you can do to prepare your classroom for digital-age learning.

What Are Some Staff-Development Ideas?

Be creative in your pursuit of ongoing staff development. If you are pressed for time, observe other teachers who use technology in their classrooms. (Ask your principal, department head, or coach to find someone to cover your classroom so you can do this.) If you are fortunate enough to have a coach or staff-development person in your building or district, ask them to set up a weekly meeting with you to work on technology goals. If you do not have a coach, partner up with another teacher or two. Peer coaching, team teaching, peer modeling, or even just conferring with other teachers is a great way to advance your goals, objectives, and outcomes.

There are many conferences and workshops offered throughout the year. Check to see if your district will cover the expenses and provide substitutes so you and your colleagues can attend. Check out the **Bureau of Education & Research (BER) (www. ber.org)**; they are a sponsor of staff-development training for professional educators in the United States and Canada, offering many technology workshops and seminars about how to implement technology with the Common Core. There are also many technology grants offered by businesses. The magazines **Innovation & Tech Today (http://innotechtoday.com)** and **Tech & Learning (www.techlearning.com)** are good places to look for these opportunities.

Ask your principal to provide grade-level time for teachers to look at standards and plan how technology can be used. Then, as a group, develop activities, projects, and lessons that include technology; come up with management strategies for using technology; and (perhaps most important) decide how you are going to assess and evaluate students' learning. This team time is so important for you to brainstorm, share and develop ideas, and gather materials. Summer is also a good time for you and your colleagues to get together to collaborate and develop projects. Check with your district to see if they will provide paid time for your summer work.

Don't forget to share your own successes and those of others. Share disappointments as well so that others can learn from them. Take pictures, write press releases, post on your school's website, and include what you are doing in your parent newsletters and emails. If possible, make a short presentation at a school board meeting. Who knows? You may gain the moral and financial support you're looking for! Share your successes any way you can.

Because needs continually change, keep planning and re-evaluating where you are and where you want to be. Encourage teachers to reach for the stars with their technology needs. Ask students how they feel about using technology and how it has affected their learning. These suggestions will help you and your colleagues get the technology you need.

Where Can You Learn about Staff Development?

There are a multitude of professional-development opportunities out there for technology, either in the workshop/conference format or online (accessible from the comfort of your home or classroom). Some opportunities are free, and some come with a membership fee to use the website or attend organization events. Others are priced per event. Following are a few suggestions.

- **ISTE (iste.org)** has several fantastic staff-development resources, including its Professional Learning Networks (PLNs), which allow you to instantly connect with experts in your field from around the globe **(http://connect.iste.org/home)**. There are many different networks to join (depending on your professional interests) where you can ask questions, learn from colleagues, and get access to exclusive events and professional learning opportunities. ISTE also offers free Strategic Learning Programs with partners like NASA and Verizon, which can be brought to your school or district **(http://bit.ly/1PeJ97t)**. In addition, ISTE may have affiliate organizations in your area that provide professional development at seminars and conferences **(iste.org/affiliates)**.

- **EdTechTeacher (http://edtechteacher.org)** is another organization that provides help to teachers and schools wishing to integrate technology to create student-centered, inquiry-based learning environments. They offer keynote presentations, hands-on workshops, online courses, and live webinars for teachers, schools, and school districts—all from your computer! What is nice about EdTechTeacher is that they understand teachers and students because the people leading the professional development have been or still are in the classroom.

- **Education World (www.educationworld.com)** is a complete online resource that offers high-quality lesson plans, classroom materials, information on how to integrate technology in the classroom, as well as articles written by education experts—a great place for you to find and share ideas with other teachers.

- **Discovery Education (www.discoveryeducation.com)** supplies a plethora of digital media that is immersive and engaging, bringing the world into the classroom to give every student a chance to experience fascinating people, places, and events. All of its content is aligned to standards that can be adjusted to support your specific curriculum and classroom instruction, regardless of what technology you have in your room. Discovery Education can help you transition to a digital-age environment and even replace all of your textbooks with digital resources, if that is your ultimate goal.

Because you are reading this book, you have already started your technology journey! And you are not alone in this nationwide endeavor. Kristi Meeuwse, an Apple Distinguished Educator, offers sage advice at her blog, **iTeach with iPads (http://ite-achwithipads.net)**, as you begin your exciting learning adventure. You can also read about **"How Kristi Meeuwse Teaches with iPad"** at Apple.com **(http://tinyurl.com/qxzdsbu)**. Following is just a taste of her guidance.

"Wherever you are in your classroom journey, it's important to reflect on where you are and where you've been. It's important to celebrate your successes, no matter how small, and then be willing to move forward and try new things. Daring to imagine the possibilities and being willing to change is not just transforming to your own teaching, it will transform your classroom in ways you never thought were possible. Today we will do exciting new things. Let's get to it."

—Kristi Meeuwse (2013, http://tinyurl.com/qf22zo7)

We will continue to give you more resources for staff development in the practical ideas chapters (8-10). To learn about staff development in grades other than 6-8, look for the three other titles in this series, as they provide information to help you differentiate for students at all levels of your class. Before we dive into lesson ideas for your specific grade and subjects, however, we will discuss how to effectively read, understand, and use the CCSS standards in the next three chapters.

Chapter 5

Organization of the Standards

So your state or district has implemented CCSS, and you are asking, "Now what? How can I make this instructional shift, understand these targets, and provide quality instruction for my students?"

You can't make this transition if you don't know your way around the CCSS. So let's focus on the first task: understanding the organization of the standards. While reading this chapter, you might want to explore **"Read the Standards"** on the CCSS website **(www.corestandards.org/read-the-standards)** as we discuss the details.

How Are the ELA Standards Organized?

The English language arts (ELA) standards for grades 6–12 are divided into seven parts (see Figure 5.1), five of which are comprehensive K–12 sections (grey boxes). Then there are two content area sections specific to grades 6–12 (white boxes): one set for literacy skills in history/social studies and one set for science/technical subjects. (The CCSS website's introduction to the ELA standards has its own **"How to Read the Standards"** section **(http://tinyurl.com/p9zfnwo)** that gives more information about organization as well as three appendices of supplemental material.)

FIGURE 5.1. The CCSS English language arts standards

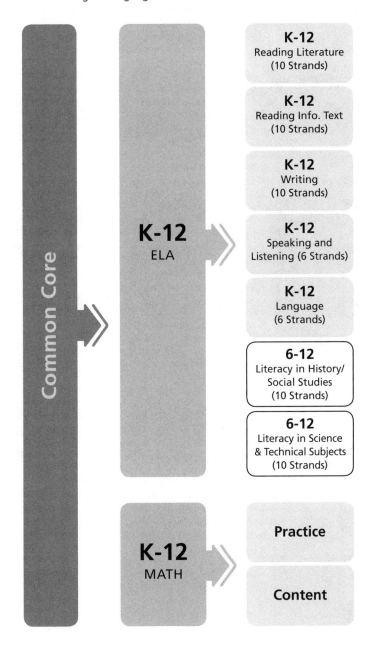

FIGURE 5.2. College and Career Readiness (CCR) anchor standard ELA 1 (CCSS.ELA-Literacy. CCRA.R.1) with grade-specific standards for Grades 6 and 8

ELA Strand → **ELA 1**
LITERACY KEY IDEAS AND DETAILS

College and Career Readiness Anchor Standard (CCRA) → **ELA 1-CCRA**
Read closely to determine what the text says explicitly and to make logical inferences from it; cite specific textual evidence when writing or speaking to support conclusions drawn from text

ELA 1 Grade Specific Standard →

Grade 6 (ELA RL.6.1)
Cite textual evidence to support analysis of what the text says explicitly as well as inferences drawn from the text.

Grade 8 (ELA RL.8.1)
Cite textual evidence that most strongly supports an analysis of what the text says explicitly as well as inferences drawn from the text.

Each section is divided into strands. At the beginning of each strand is a set of College and Career Readiness (CCR) anchor standards, which are the same across all grades and content areas. Take, for example, the first anchor standard illustrated in Figure 5.2: ELA 1 (CCSS.ELA-Literacy.CCRA.R.1). It is the same in grade 6 as it is for an eighth grader, but the grade-level standard is refined to what the student at each grade level is expected to accomplish within the anchor standard.

ELA 1 Anchor Standard: Read closely to determine what the text says explicitly and to make logical inferences from it; cite specific textual evidence when writing or speaking to support conclusions drawn from the text.

ELA 1 Standard in Grade 6: Cite textual evidence to support analysis of what the text says explicitly as well as inferences drawn from the text.

ELA 1 Standard in Grade 8: Cite textual evidence that most strongly supports an analysis of what the text says explicitly as well as inferences drawn from the text.

These anchor standards compliment the specific grade-level standards and define the skills knowledge base that students should have by the end of each grade. The CCR standards are broad, while the grade-level standards provide specificity.

ELA standards focus on the following four areas:

1. Reading

2. Writing

3. Speaking and Listening

4. Language

The reading standards focus on text complexity (the difficulty of what students read), as well as the growth of their comprehension skills. Along with fictional stories and informational text, the CCSS focuses on poetry and dramas too. The writing standards delve into specific text types, reading response, and research. Some writing skills such as the ability to plan, revise, edit, and publish can be applied to most types of writing. Other writing skills are more specific: opinion and argumentation; informational explanatory texts, and narratives. Speaking and listening standards deal with collaboration and flexible communication. In this area, students acquire and refine their oral communication and interpersonal skills, perhaps through formal presentations.

The language standards concentrate on vocabulary, conventions, and effective use. This strand not only incorporates the essential "rules" of standard written and spoken English but also helps students to understand how language functions in different contexts. Making effective choices in meaning and style leads to better comprehension when reading and listening. The vocabulary part of this strand clarifies and/or determines the meaning of unknown and multiple-definition words and phrases by using the appropriate context clues and/or reference materials as needed. This strand also helps students demonstrate an understanding of figurative language, word relationships, and nuances in word meanings. In addition, students will be able to acquire and accurately use a range of general and domain-specific words and phrases in any academic area. (We'll talk more about domains later in this chapter, in the math standards section.)

With the organization in mind, let's learn how you, as an individual teacher, use the CCSS in ELA.

How Do You Find ELA Standards by Subject and Grade?

Since most middle school teachers teach just one or two subjects, the standards are organized so that you can focus on your specific area. But it is very helpful to look back at the level before you and look ahead to the standards that come next, to put your grade-level curriculum in context. (If you would like to look at a grade not included in this book, please refer to the other titles in this series.)

Using the main "English Language Arts Standards" page on the CCSS website is probably the most efficient way to find your grade- and subject-level standards **(www.corestandards.org/ELA-Literacy)**. If you know what you are looking for, the corresponding reference numbers are useful. Here is a quick introduction:

All standards that relate to literature, informational text, writing, speaking, listening, language, history/social studies, and science and technical begin with "CCSS. ELA-Literacy." The difference comes at the end, with the numbering system.

Let's use the following as an example.

CCSS.ELA-Literacy.RL.7.1

- **CCSS** is the abbreviation for Common Core State Standard.

- **ELA-Literacy** identifies this as an English language arts standard.

- **RL** stands for "reading literature."

- **7** is the grade.

- **1** is the strand.

CCSS.ELA-Literacy.RH.6-8.5

- **CCSS.ELA-Literacy** represents the same information as in the previous example.

- **RH** means "reading history."

- **6-8** is the grade range.

- **5** is the strand.

But there are standards within standards that are not easily apparent at first glance. For instance, there may be a reading standard that uses historical or science text, or a speaking-and-listening standard that has a technology component to it. This book focuses on where technology is required in the CCSS, and there is plenty of technology to discuss in ELA and math!

You may be wondering how you will be able to keep all of this straight. After all, we haven't even started talking about math! We invite you to go online to view the math standards (www.corestandards.org/Math) as you read this next section.

How Does the Organization of Math Standards Differ?

When you look at the math standards, you will see immediately that they were written by a different group of individuals; they do not integrate other subjects like the ELA standards. Even the technology standard is separate. And the system of organization is different too. The authors of the standards also state that the grade-level order can be changed. After the following overview, we will help you sort it all out.

For more than a decade, it has been widely reported that math curriculum in the United States is not even close to being on the same level as math education in high-performing countries. The consensus: U.S. math education needs to become substantially more focused and coherent to improve. To solve this, the CCSS were written to be clear, specific, and rigorous. Not only do the Common Core math standards stress conceptual understanding of key ideas but they continually return to the main organizing principles (place value and properties of operations) to structure those ideas. It is important to note that these new standards address what students should understand and be able to do in their study of mathematics. But asking a student to understand something also means asking a teacher to assess whether a student understands it. Therefore, we need to break apart these standards to enhance readability and to gauge what Common Core math comprehension looks like—so your students will be able to understand and you will be able to assess.

First, you need to understand that the standards provide a solid foundation in basic math before middle school. In grades 6-8, the study of ratios, proportions, and algebra is where the major math focus falls. Instead of covering a myriad of topics, your students will be required to immerse themselves in deep comprehension by applying mathematics to problems they have not encountered previously.

The CCSS for math begin with eight Standards for **Mathematical Practice (SMP) (www.corestandards.org/Math/Practice)**, which apply to all grades, K-12. These standards represent ways in which students will be engaged with math content, processes, and proficiencies—longstanding, important practices. The eight SMP are:

1. Make sense of problems and persevere in solving them.

2. Reason abstractly and quantitatively.

3. Construct viable arguments and critique the reasoning of others.

4. Model with mathematics.

5. Use appropriate tools strategically.

6. Attend to precision.

7. Look for and make use of structure.

8. Look for and express regularity in repeated reasoning.

For kindergarten through eighth grade, there are also grade-specific standards. Each contains a number of domains. Domains are larger groups of related standards that are sometimes broken into clusters. Clusters are summarized groups of related standards that fall under the main standard (see the cluster that follows the standard in Figure 5.3). Due to the connected nature of math, you may see closely related clusters in other domains as well. You can read more about this on the "How to Read Grade-Level Standards" page of the CCSS website's math standards intro-duction at http://bit.ly/1sPykwd.

The grade-specific domains for Grades 6–8 are the following:

- Ratios and Proportional Relationships (6 and 7 only)

- The Number System (6-8)

- Expressions and Equations (6-8)

- Functions (8 only)

- Geometry (K-8)

- Statistics and Probability (6-8)

Here is an example of how domains are used to organize the math standards:

CCSS.Math.Content.8.EE.A.1

- **CCSS** is the abbreviation for Common Core State Standards.

- **Math.Content** identifies that this is a math standard.

- **8.EE** is the domain (Grade 8–Expressions and Equations).

- **A.1** is the identifier for a related standard (or cluster) under the main stan-dard–in this case "Expressions and equations work with radicals and integer exponents" (see Figure 5.3).

Now that you know how to identify a math standard and its numbering system, let's look at the following figure to see the way in which this standard is actually pre-sented in this domain.

TABLE 5.3. Figure 5.3. Example of a standard in the eighth grade domain of Expressions and Equations

DOMAIN	STANDARD	CLUSTER
Grade 8 **Expressions and Equations**	Expressions and equations work with radicals and integer exponents.	**CCSS.Math.Content.8.EE.A.1:** Know and apply the properties of integer exponents to generate equivalent numerical expressions. For example, 32 x 3-5 = 3-3 = 1/33 = 1/27. **CCSS.Math.Content.8.EE.A.2:** Use square root and cube root symbols to represent solutions to equations of the form x2 = p and x3 = p, where p is a positive rational number. Evaluate square roots of small perfect squares and cube roots of small perfect cubes. Know that √2 is irrational. **CCSS.Math.Content.8.EE.A.3:** Use numbers expressed in the form of a single digit times an integer power of 10 to estimate very large or very small quantities, and to express how many times as much one is than the other. For example: estimate the population of the United States as 3 times 108 and the population of the world as 7 times 109, and determine that the world population is more than 20 times larger. **CCSS.Math.Content.8.EE.A.4:** Perform operations with numbers expressed in scientific notation, including problems where both decimal and scientific notation are used. Use scientific notation and choose units of appropriate size for measurements of very large or very small quantities (e.g., use millimeters per year for seafloor spreading). Interpret scientific notation that has been generated by technology.

The standard in Figure 5.3 defines what your students should know and be able to do after you have taught and assessed that standard. Reading and familiarizing yourself with the standards will go a long way in helping you teach the standards later.

There are also SMPs that are part of the College and Career Readiness (CCR) anchor standards of the ELA. These standards are not overtly assessed but are necessary for you to include in your instruction. SMPs will not be the focus of this book except when they involve technology.

As you can see, math and ELA standards are written and organized very differently. We have tried our best to guide you through these differences, but we do recommend that you explore the resources we have provided here as well as others that we have referenced on **our website (http://tinyurl.com/oexfhcv)**. Here are two great resources that will explain the standards of mathematical practices: **http://tinyurl.com/l3zzsae, http://tinyurl.com/9ndshh6**. In the next chapter, we discuss technology and how it relates to the CCSS.

Chapter 6

Technology in the Common Core

This chapter focuses on the CCSS English language arts and math standards that have technology-related components written into them, first identifying and then analyzing these standards. This will prepare you for the later chapters, where we offer practical examples of how you can integrate these standards into your curriculum.

As CCSS coaches, we know that there are those of you who are excited about technology, those of you who think it is an annoyance, and those of you who fear it. These new standards will affect all of you because they force your districts and you, as teachers, to use technology more pervasively. Schools will feel pressure to address areas that may have been avoided in the past because of cost or apprehension. If you are a fan of technology, you will welcome the changes; if you are not, you will need to become proficient. You can no longer avoid technology in your classroom.

Where Is Technology in the ELA Standards?

The CCSS are designed to prepare students for college, the workforce, and a technology-rich society. And as you learned in the last chapter, the ELA standards have

ELA Standards (Grades 6–8) in Which Technology Appears

READING (6–8)

- CCR Reading (R) Standard 7 **(http://tinyurl.com/h9n9ek9)**.
  - Reading Literature (RL)
  - Reading Informational Text (RI)
  - Reading History (RH)

- CCR Reading Science and Technical Subjects (RST) Standard 9 **(http://tinyurl.com/jylor72)**.

Note: While reading language (RL) and reading informational text (RI) are in all grades, reading history (RH) and reading science and technical subjects (RST) are in Grades 6-12 only. We will get into more detail about this and related anchor standard R.9 later in this chapter.

WRITING (6–8)

- CCR Writing (W) Standard 2 **(http://tinyurl.com/zt6kysv)**.
  - Writing, History, Science, and Technical Subjects (WHST) Standard 2

- CCR Writing (W) Standard 6 **(http://tinyurl.com/zmxfdp8)**.
  - Writing, History, Science, and Technical Subjects (WHST) Standard 6

- CCR Writing (W) Standard 8 **(http://tinyurl.com/jercjbv)**.
  - Writing, History, Science, and Technical Subjects (WHST) Standard 8

Note: Writing is an anchor standard throughout students' K-12 education, but an added strand of history, science, and technical subjects (WHST) is included from Grades 6-12.

SPEAKING AND LISTENING (6–8)

- CCR Speaking and Listening (SL) Standard 2 **(http://tinyurl.com/gvdrr3g)**.
- CCR Speaking and Listening (SL) Standard 5 **(http://tinyurl.com/hrw3bdu)**.

LANGUAGE (6–8)

- CCR Language (L) Standard 4 **(http://tinyurl.com/hmu54nx)**.

the CCR (College and Career Readiness) anchor standards—writing, reading, speaking and listening, and language—at their core. Following is a summary of those CCR standards that are embedded with technology in Grades 6–8.

Where Is Technology in the Math Standards?

As mentioned in Chapter 5, the math standards are written differently, and the technology standard in math (yes, just one standard) is separate from the rest of the math standards. However, this technology standard is meant to be used ubiquitously. Though many math standards do not overtly say that technology is required, if there is a need for a calculator or statistical analysis using a computer then that is what students should use. In math, the understanding is that these technology tools are used across grade levels and throughout the math standards even though there is only one written standard about it. (Note: See this math standard presented in detail after the grade-specific ELA standards at the end of this chapter.)

What about Using Technology in All Subjects?

Because technology is integrated throughout the CCSS, we should discuss in more depth what this actually means as you go about implementing the curriculum day to day. Though the standards give you specific language, the use of technology has been left wide open. They use terms like "digital tools," "other media," and "both print and digital" to let you, as the teacher, choose what is appropriate to the lesson. The new standards are trying to infuse technology into everyday classroom use, as opposed to having a separate period in a computer lab. Technology will need to become like the pencil: just another tool to choose from when students need to find the most appropriate one to complete the task at hand.

CCSS strongly encourages project-based lessons and is built to be cross-curricular. Also, Common Core is looking for higher-level thinking, learning, and application. All of these things lead to the use of technology as the most appropriate tool in many situations. They fit very well into P21's (Partnership for 21st Century Learning's) **Framework for 21st Century Learning (http://tinyurl.com/nzvwyen)** and the **ISTE Standards for Students (www.iste.org/standards)**. So if you have been working for some time on lessons that integrate technology and you think you will have to begin again, you will be relieved to know that the new standards are not so different.

How Do You Put ELA Technology Standards into Context?

When you look at the patterns of technology use in the standards you improve your integration planning and learning achievements with these standards. Let's take a quick look at the technology patterns in the related Grade 6–8 standards.

R.7: This is the main technology standard in reading, but the CCSS does not expect students to use technology until Grade 2. The standard then continues to develop in all subsequent grades, integrating and evaluating content in various technology formats that support the meaning of a story or literary work.

> **RL.7:** This standard begins in kindergarten, comparing illustrations and text, and then grows through the grades, using all types of media to compare, support, and analyze the story's meaning. Essentially, the purpose of the standard is to get meaning from more than the text. Meaning can also come from all the accompanying media and even the format of the story.

> **RI.7, RH.7:** These are similar to RL.7 but refer to informational text, history, and science and technical subjects. Thus, you must keep in mind informational graphics—maps; photographs; diagrams; charts; and other media in history, technical subjects, and science—and the way in which they augment information or help to solve a problem.

RST.9: This standard begins in Grades 6–8 with specific technology suggested, and it implies technology use in Grades 9–12. Students are asked to compare science and technical information they have studied with what they experience through experiments, simulations, videos, and other media, to build knowledge.

W.2: From drawing, writing, and telling about a topic in kindergarten, this standard evolves into producing a thesis in high school. It is your basic research paper that now includes an expectation to use any and all media that is appropriate to conveying the information.

W.6: This is one of the few anchor standards that is solely technology driven. From kindergarten through high school, students are required to use technology to collaborate with others when writing. Of course, this requires keyboarding skills, but they are not mentioned in the standard until Grade 3.

W.8: The use of technology in this standard is expected from Grade 3 through high school. It keys in on the gathering of information, the analysis of information, and the avoidance of plagiarism using multiple sources—digital as well as text—when writing informative or explanatory works. This standard works in tandem with standard W.2 and will probably be taught jointly.

> **WHST.2, WHST.6, WHST.8:** These Grade 6–12 writing standards are similar to their W.2, W.6, and W.8 anchors, but the focus is on history, science, and technology and the use of multimedia tools.

SL.2: This standard expects the use of technology from kindergarten through Grade 12. It is a listening standard, but in today's world, all kinds of diverse media are constantly available. Students need to be able to analyze and make decisions about this content.

SL.5: Beginning with the use of pictures when speaking in kindergarten, this standard builds to making strategic use of digital media for presentations in high school. Learning to use media in presentations is critical for college and career readiness.

L.4: This is a very straightforward standard that clarifies the meaning of words at all grade levels. Starting in second grade, students need to know how to find word meanings using not just print but digital dictionaries, glossaries, and thesauruses.

What about Assessment?

You don't begin a trip without an end in mind, and the end that must always be kept in mind with the CCSS is the standardized test your state will be administering. Whether it is the PARCC or Smarter Balanced assessment, or some other assessment your state is developing, there will certainly be a technology component to it. The tests will require some level of competence in selecting and highlighting text, dragging and dropping text, and moving objects on the screen. In the math areas of the test, tools that might be needed for the exam (calculators, rulers, a slide rule) will be available on the screen. Students may need headphones and a microphone to interact during the speaking-and-listening sections, and other multimedia may be used in other parts of the test.

The best way to prepare students is to know in advance the scope of technology they will need to master, but this will not be easy during the first years of rollout. Many things will be changing and many details will still be forthcoming. The tight deadline means your students may not be as fully prepared as you would like them to be. However, your preparation—giving students opportunities to use a myriad of technology as often as possible—will help them to be as ready as they can be for the assessments.

What Are the ELA Standards with Technology?

The following is a listing of where technology appears in the CCSS. The first section contains the anchor standards, and the second section has the more specific grade-level standards. The standards are in order by level so that you can find those that relate to the grade you teach more quickly. The part of the standard that pertains to technology is in boldface type. It is always helpful to look at the standards above and below your level to see where the students have come from and where they are going on their educational journey. Please refer to the other books in this series if you would like to see other grade levels.

READING
CCSS.ELA-Literacy.CCRA.R.7

R.7: Integrate and evaluate content presented in **diverse media and formats**, including visually and quantitatively, as well as in words.

Note R.9 as well: Analyze how two or more texts address similar themes or topics in order to build knowledge or to compare the approaches the authors take.

The R.9 anchor standard does not have any multimedia but does overtly include technology in its science and technical strand concerning the use of simulations, videos, and multimedia sources in Grades 6–8 (**RST.6-8.9**).

WRITING
CCSS.ELA-Literacy.CCRA.W.6 and CCSS.ELA-Literacy.CCRA.W.8

W.6: Use technology, including the internet, to produce and publish writing and to interact and collaborate with others.

W.8: Gather relevant information from multiple print and **digital sources**, assess the credibility and accuracy of each source, and integrate the information while avoiding plagiarism.

Note: Anchor standard **W.2** does not have multimedia but does include technology in that standard's strand starting in Grade 4 (**W.4.2.a**). This book focuses on **W.5.2.a**, **W.6.2.a**, **W.7.2.a**, **W.8.2.a**.

SPEAKING AND LISTENING

CCSS.ELA-Literacy.CCRA.SL.2 and CCSS.ELA-Literacy.CCRA.SL.5

SL.2: Integrate and evaluate information presented in **diverse media and formats**, including visually, quantitatively, and orally.

SL.5: Make strategic use of **digital media** and **visual displays** of data to express information and enhance understanding of presentations.

Even when your grade does not have a technology standard included in these main anchor strands (**R.7**, **W.2**, **W.6**, **W.8**, **SL.2**, **SL.5**, **L.4**), it is implied that it be used. We have listed here only those that state a technology use.

What are the ELA Grade-Level Standards with Technology?

Following is where ELA grade-level standards appear in the CCSS (listed by grade). Note the following abbreviations: reading literature (RL), reading informational text (RI), writing (W), speaking and listening (SL), and language (L). We are including one grade below and above to give the technology standards some context. Please refer to the other books in this series to get a sense of the full scope of technology standards, Grades K–12. (Note: As in the preceding section, the part of the standard that pertains to technology is in boldface type.)

GRADE 5

RL.5.7: Analyze how visual and **multimedia elements** contribute to the meaning, tone, or beauty of a text (e.g., graphic novel, **multimedia presentation** of fiction, folktale, myth, poem).

RI.5.7: Draw on information from multiple print or **digital sources**, demonstrating the ability to locate an answer to a question quickly or to solve a problem efficiently.

W.5.2.a: Introduce a topic clearly, provide a general observation and focus, and group related information logically; include formatting (e.g., headings), illustrations, and **multimedia** when useful to aiding comprehension.

W.5.6: With some guidance and support from adults, **use technology, including the internet**, to produce and publish writing as well as to interact and collaborate with others; demonstrate sufficient command of **keyboarding skills** to type a minimum of two pages in a single sitting.

W.5.8: Recall relevant information from experiences or gather relevant information from print and **digital sources**; summarize or paraphrase information in notes and finished work, and provide a list of sources.

SL.5.2: Summarize a written text read aloud or information presented in **diverse media and formats**, including visually, quantitatively, and orally.

SL.5.5: Include **multimedia components (e.g., graphics, sound)** and **visual displays** in presentations when appropriate to enhance the development of main ideas or themes.

L.5.4.c: Consult reference materials (e.g., dictionaries, glossaries, thesauruses), both print and **digital**, to find the pronunciation and determine or clarify the precise meaning of key words and phrases.

GRADE 6

RL.6.7: Compare and contrast the experience of reading a story, drama, or poem to listening to or viewing an **audio, video**, or live version of the text, including contrasting what they "see" and "hear" when reading the text to what they perceive when they listen or watch.

RI.6.7: Integrate information presented in **different media or formats** (e.g., visually, quantitatively) as well as in words to develop a coherent understanding of a topic or issue.

RH.6-8.7: Integrate visual information (e.g., in charts, graphs, photographs, **videos**, or maps) with other information in print and **digital texts**.

RST.6-8.9: Compare and contrast the information gained from experiments, **simulations, video, or multimedia sources** with that gained from reading a text on the same topic.

W.6.2.a: Introduce a topic; organize ideas, concepts, and information, using strategies such as definition, classification, comparison/contrast, and cause/effect; include formatting (e.g., headings), graphics (e.g., charts, tables), and **multimedia** when useful to aiding comprehension.

W.6.6: Use technology, including the internet, to produce and publish writing as well as to interact and collaborate with others; demonstrate sufficient command of keyboarding skills to type a minimum of three pages in a single sitting.

W.6.8: Gather relevant information from multiple print and **digital sources**; assess the credibility of each source; and quote or paraphrase the data and conclusions of others while avoiding plagiarism and providing basic bibliographic information for sources.

WHST.6-8.2.a: Introduce a topic clearly, previewing what is to follow; organize ideas, concepts, and information into broader categories as appropriate to achieving purpose; include formatting (e.g., headings), graphics (e.g., charts, tables), and **multimedia** when useful to aiding comprehension.

WHST.6-8.6: Use technology, including the internet, to produce and publish writing and present the relationships between information and ideas clearly and efficiently.

SL.6.2: Interpret information presented in **diverse media and formats** (e.g., visually, quantitatively, orally) and explain how it contributes to a topic, text, or issue under study.

SL.6.5: Include **multimedia** components (e.g., graphics, images, music, sound) and **visual displays** in presentations to clarify information.

L.6.4.c: Consult reference materials (e.g., dictionaries, glossaries, thesauruses), both print and **digital**, to find the pronunciation of a word or to determine or clarify its precise meaning or its part of speech.

GRADE 7

RL.7.7: Compare and contrast a written story, drama, or poem to its audio, filmed, staged, or **multimedia version**, analyzing the effects of techniques unique to each medium (e.g., lighting, sound, color, or camera focus and angles in a film).

RI.7.7: Compare and contrast a text to an audio, video, or **multimedia** version of the text, analyzing each medium's portrayal of the subject (e.g., how the delivery of a speech affects the impact of the words).

RH.6-8.7: Integrate visual information (e.g., in charts, graphs, photographs, videos, or maps) with other information in print and **digital texts**.

RST.6-8.9: Compare and contrast the information gained from experiments, **simulations, video, or multimedia sources** with that gained from reading a text on the same topic.

W.7.2.a: Introduce a topic clearly, previewing what is to follow; organize ideas, concepts, and information, using strategies such as definition, classification, comparison/contrast, and cause/effect; include formatting (e.g., headings), graphics (e.g., charts, tables), and **multimedia** when useful to aiding comprehension.

W.7.6: Use technology, including the internet, to produce and publish writing and link to and cite sources as well as to interact and collaborate with others, including linking to and citing sources.

W.7.8 and **WHST.6-8.8**: Gather relevant information from multiple print and **digital sources**, using search terms effectively; assess the credibility and accuracy of each source; and quote or paraphrase the data and conclusions of others while avoiding plagiarism and following a standard format for citation.

WHST.6-8.2.a: Introduce a topic clearly, previewing what is to follow; organize ideas, concepts, and information into broader categories as appropriate to achieving purpose; include formatting (e.g., headings), graphics (e.g., charts, tables), and **multimedia** when useful to aiding comprehension.

WHST.6-8.6: Use technology, including the internet, to produce and publish writing, and present the relationships between information and ideas clearly and efficiently.

SL.7.2: Analyze the main ideas and supporting details presented in **diverse media and formats** (e.g., visually, quantitatively, and orally) and explain how the ideas clarify a topic, text, or issue under study.

SL.7.5: Include **multimedia components** and **visual displays** in presentations to clarify claims and findings, and emphasize salient points.

L.7.4.c: Consult general and specialized reference materials (e.g., dictionaries, glossaries, thesauruses), both print and **digital**, to find the pronunciation of a word or to determine or clarify its precise meaning or its part of speech.

GRADE 8

RL.8.7: Analyze the extent to which a **filmed** or live production of a story or drama stays faithful to or departs from the text or script, evaluating the choices made by the director or actors.

RI.8.7: Evaluate the advantages and disadvantages of using different mediums (e.g., print or **digital text, video, multimedia**) to present a particular topic or idea.

RH.6-8.7: Integrate visual information (e.g., in charts, graphs, photographs, videos, or maps) with other information in print and **digital texts**.

RST.6-8.9: Compare and contrast the information gained from experiments, **simulations, video, or multimedia sources** with that gained from reading a text on the same topic.

W.8.2.a: Introduce a topic clearly, previewing what is to follow; organize ideas, concepts, and information into broader categories; include formatting (e.g., headings), graphics (e.g., charts, tables), and **multimedia** when useful to aiding comprehension.

W.8.6: Use technology, including the internet, to produce and publish writing and present the relationships between information and ideas efficiently as well as to interact and collaborate with others **(www.corestandards.org/ELA-Literacy/W/8/6)**.

W.8.8 and **WHST.6-8.8**: Gather relevant information from multiple print and **digital sources**, using search terms effectively; assess the credibility and accuracy of each source; and quote or paraphrase the data and conclusions of others while avoiding plagiarism and following a standard format for citation.

WHST.6-8.2.a: Introduce a topic clearly, previewing what is to follow; organize ideas, concepts, and information into broader categories as appropriate to achieving purpose; include formatting (e.g., headings), graphics (e.g., charts, tables), and **multimedia** when useful to aiding comprehension.

WHST.6-8.6: Use technology, including the internet, to produce and publish writing and present the relationships between information and ideas clearly and efficiently.

SL.8.2: Analyze the purpose of information presented in **diverse media and formats** (e.g., visually, quantitatively, orally) and evaluate the motives (e.g., social, commercial, political) behind its presentation.

SL.8.5: Integrate **multimedia and visual displays** into presentations to clarify information, strengthen claims and evidence, and add interest.

L.8.4.c: Consult general and specialized reference materials (e.g., dictionaries, glossaries, thesauruses), both print and **digital**, to find the pronunciation of a word or to determine or clarify its precise meaning or its part of speech.

GRADES 9–10

RL.9-10.7: Analyze the representation of a subject or a key scene in **two different artistic mediums**, including what is emphasized or absent in each treatment (e.g., Auden's Musée des Beaux Arts and Breughel's Landscape with the Fall of Icarus).

RI.9-10.7: Analyze various accounts of a subject told in **different mediums** (e.g., a person's life story in both print and **multimedia**), determining which details are emphasized in each account.

RH.9-10.7: Integrate quantitative or technical analysis (e.g., charts, research data) with qualitative analysis in print or **digital text**.

RST.9-10.7: Translate quantitative or technical information expressed in words in a text into **visual form** (e.g., a table or chart) and translate information expressed visually or mathematically (e.g., in an equation) into words.

RST.9-10.9: Compare and contrast findings presented in a text to those from **other sources** (including their own experiments), noting when the findings support or contradict previous explanations or accounts.

W.9-10.2.a and **WHST.9-10.2.a**: Introduce a topic; organize complex ideas, concepts, and information to make important connections and distinctions; include formatting (e.g., headings), graphics (e.g., figures, tables), and **multimedia** when useful to aiding comprehension.

W.9-10.6 and **WHST.9-10.6**: **Use technology, including the internet**, to produce, publish, and update individual or shared writing products, taking advantage of technology's capacity to link to other information and to display information flexibly and dynamically.

W.9-10.8. and **WHST.9-10.8**: Gather relevant information from multiple authoritative print and **digital sources**, using advanced searches effectively; assess the usefulness of each source in answering the research question; integrate information into the text selectively to maintain the flow of ideas, avoiding plagiarism and following a standard format for citation.

SL.9-10.2: Integrate multiple sources of information presented in **diverse media or formats** (e.g., visually, quantitatively, orally) evaluating the credibility and accuracy of each source.

SL.9-10.5: Make strategic use of **digital media** (e.g., textual, **graphical, audio, visual, and interactive elements**) in presentations to enhance understanding of findings, reasoning, and evidence, and to add interest.

L.9-10.4.c: Consult general and specialized reference materials (e.g., dictionaries, glossaries, thesauruses), both print and **digital**, to find the pronunciation of a word or to determine or clarify its precise meaning, its part of speech, or its etymology.

What Is the Math Standard with Technology?

The Standards for Mathematical Practice (SMP) are skills that all of your students should look to develop. As you learned in Chapter 5, there are eight SMP, which are designed to overlay the math content standards. In other words, the math practice standards apply to every one of the math content standards. So, although **MP5** is the only standard that includes technology, it actually means that every math content standard should use the appropriate tools, including tools that use technology.

Following is **MP5**, taken verbatim from the Common Core State Standards website. As in the preceding two sections, any text that pertains to technology is in boldface type.

CCSS.MATH.PRACTICE.MP5

MP5. Use appropriate **tools** strategically.

Mathematically proficient students consider the available tools when solving a mathematical problem. These tools might include pencil and paper, concrete models, a ruler, a protractor, **a calculator, a spreadsheet, a computer algebra system, a statistical package, or dynamic geometry software**. Proficient students are sufficiently familiar with tools appropriate for their grade or course to make sound decisions about when each of these tools might be helpful, recognizing both the insight to be gained and their limitations. For example, mathematically proficient high school students analyze graphs of functions and solutions generated using a **graphing calculator**. They detect possible errors by strategically using estimation and other mathematical knowledge. When making mathematical models, they know that **technology** can enable them to visualize the results of varying assumptions, explore consequences, and compare predictions with data. Mathematically proficient students at various grade levels are able to identify relevant external mathematical resources, such as **digital content located on a website**, and use them to pose or solve problems. They are able to use **technological tools** to explore and deepen their understanding of concepts.

It is important to note the standard's emphasis on using technology pervasively. Keep technology in mind, not only when teaching the standards but in the assessment, as it creates a learning advantage for your students.

We hope you have taken away important information on where technology can be found in the CCSS. In the next chapter, we discuss practical strategies and offer helpful resources so you can begin teaching the CCSS right away.

Chapter 7

Implementing Practical Ideas

O ur world and education is changing rapidly. Without question, one size does not fit all in teaching. We know you work hard to personalize the learning in your classroom to reflect the individual needs, capabilities, and learning styles of your students so they have opportunities to reach their maximum potential. With this in mind, why not create tech-savvy classrooms for today's students?

In this chapter, we address practical ways to use new technology ideas within your classroom. Most of your students already come to school with a strong background in and understanding of technology. They are interested, motivated, and even driven by technology. Having a tech-savvy classroom for today's students is the best way to create a digital-age learning environment.

How and Where Do I Begin?

Whether you are a new teacher, a teacher in the middle of a career, or a veteran teacher with just a few years before retirement, you will begin at the same place in respect to technology. To bring technology into your classrooms and your students into the digital age, you must give up your role at the front of class and let technology be a primary source of information. This journey calls for no longer teaching in the way you've been teaching and instead becoming facilitators of your classroom and the information presented there. Embrace all of the devices you have ignored or struggled to keep out of your classroom. Introduce yourself to new concepts that may not have existed when you were in school.

First, sign up for as many technology teaching blogs and websites as you can find. One website definitely worth a look is **Power My Learning (http://powermylearning. org)**. There are many free activities for you to explore and you can search for lessons by the CCSS. This website also allows you to build classes, assign and monitor student work, and customize playlists for your classroom.

Blogs are becoming an increasingly pervasive and persistent influence in people's lives. They are a great way to allow individual participation in the marketplace of ideas around the world. Teachers have picked up on the creative use of this technology and put the blog to work in the classroom. The education blog can be a powerful and effective tool for students and teachers. **Edutopia** has a wonderful technology blog **(http://tinyurl.com/p33sd7b)**. Scholastic also offers a blog for teachers, PK–12, **(http://tinyurl.com/oaaycar)** and on a wide variety of educational topics.

Edmodo (https://www.edmodo.com) is a free and easy blog for students and teachers to communicate back and forth. Teachers can post assignments and students can respond to the teacher, as well as to each other, either in the classroom or at home. Students have the ability to also post questions to the teacher or one another, if they need help.

What Strategies Can I Use?

Get a routine going. Engage students in independent and self-directed learning activities. This is a great way to begin integrating technology in your classroom. All activities can be tied to your curriculum targets and a couple of them can be technology based. A plethora of computer-based games exist that you can bring to a center rotation. **ScootPad (www.scootpad.com)** and **DreamBox (www.dreambox. com)** are two programs that support Common Core and can be used on computers or tablets.

Differentiated math instruction meets the needs of all learners. It consists of, whole group, mini lessons, guided math groups, and independent learning stations with a wide variety of activities, and ongoing assessment. Independent learning stations are a great way to infuse technology into your centers. One station with computers and another with games make great rotation centers and are easy to plan for, as well as a great way for students to practice math fluency and target related games. For more information on how to set up a guided math classroom check out the book *Guided Math: A Framework for Mathematics Instruction* (2009) by Laney Sammons, or view her **guided math slide presentation** online **(www.slideshare.net/ggierhart/ guided-math-powerpointbytheauthorofguidedmath)**.

Guided Reading is a key component of Balanced Literacy instruction. The teacher meets with a small group of students, reading and instructing them at their level. Other students are involved in small groups or independent practice that involves reading, writing, or vocabulary. **Reading A-Z (www.readinga-z.com)** offers many literacy-based books and games that can be used in reading centers. Students can use recording devices to record and listen to themselves reading. You can also listen to their recordings for quick assessment purposes. **Learning A-Z (www.learninga-z. com)** also offers **Vocabulary A-Z** and **Science A-Z**. There are many games and activities for these content areas, and this offers you additional rotations for your literacy centers. Programs and apps, such as Google Docs, Puppet Pals, and Comic Life, are just a few resources you can use to meet standards and bring writing into your literacy rotations while giving your students the opportunity to use technology to be creative.

Flipping the classroom is another great way to integrate technology into your classroom. This teaching model, which uses both online and face-to-face instruction, is transforming education. Flipping is an educational strategy that provides students with the chance to access information within a subject outside of the classroom. Instead of students listening in class to content and then practicing that concept outside of the school day, that traditional practice is flipped. Students work with information whenever it best fits their schedule, and as many times as necessary for learning to occur. Inside the flipped classroom, teachers and students engage in discussion, practice, or experiential learning. By creating online tutorials of your instruction, using some of the tools mentioned in this book, you can spend valuable class time assisting students with homework, conferencing about learning, or simply being available for student questions.

Pick an app or program you are interested in bringing into your classroom. Play and explore. See what the possibilities are for using this technology in your classroom. You and your students can be technology pioneers. Allow your students to problem solve and seek new knowledge on their own and then have them share with you. A great resource to use is **iPad in Education (www.apple.com/education/ ipad)**, where you can learn more about how to teach with and use iPads in your classroom. This site from Apple is a great resource—it gives you lots of information about what the iPad is capable of, gives examples of iPad lessons done by other teachers, and offers free apps!

How Do I Determine What Works Best?

Perhaps the next place to look is the **ISTE Standards for Students**, which were developed by the International Society for Technology in Education (ISTE) and can be found on their website **(www.iste.org/standards)**. These standards are a great framework to help you plan lessons and projects to support the Common Core technology standards in literacy, math, and critical thinking skills.

The Partnership for 21st Century Skills developed a Framework for 21st Century Learning. This framework identifies key skills known as the 4Cs: Critical Thinking, Collaboration, Communication, and Creativity. Table 7.1 takes those four skills and overlays them with digital resources that you can use in English language arts (ELA). For instance, if you are a seventh grade teacher and want to use Collaboration in your lesson, you might try any of the seven digital resources suggested to plan the lesson: Google Docs, Popplet, GarageBand, Wixie, Edmodo, wikis, and Google Sites. These are suggestions, but there are many more apps and sites that might also fit well. You might notice that the 4Cs mirror many of the ISTE standards. This table is included to get you to think about how you can include the 4Cs and technology in your daily lesson planning.

Being an expert on all of the apps or programs listed in Table 7.1 is not necessary. Start with one you know, or find out which ones your students are familiar with and start there. Think about the target or lesson you want to teach. What is the goal? What technology device or app or program will support your teaching? Create an end product to show your students what you expect. Instead of step-by-step

TABLE 7.1. How Digital Resources for ELA Fit into the 4C's.

GRADE	CRITICAL THINKING	COLLABORATION	COMMUNICATION	CREATIVITY
6-8	**DreamBox Learning** **Reading/Science A-Z** **WatchKnowLearn** **NeoK12**	**Google Sites** **Popplet** **GarageBand** **Edmodo** **Wikis** **Google Docs**	**Explain Everything** **Skype** **Edmodo** **Show Me** **GarageBand**	**Microsoft Office** **GarageBand** **iMovie** **Keynote**

teaching of the technology, it is important to let the students explore and discover for themselves, as long as your end product and expectations have been met.

You can also teach yourself about many of the apps or programs available by searching for them online. YouTube also has step-by-step how-to videos for many tech apps and programs. Have your students show what they know by creating samples for you. Save everything you, your colleagues, or your students create, and keep it all in a digital portfolio, so you can share the samples with your students for years to come.

With an active learning environment and providing the tools your students need for 21st-century learning, watch the difference you will make as learning in your classroom skyrockets. All of this new technology is transforming today's class-rooms. Social networking and mobile learning are just a few tech-related activities that students and teachers are embracing. **The website for this book (http://tinyurl. com/oexfhcv)** contains additional lists of resources for how to incorporate the tech-nology you have (or want to have) and ways for your students to learn and interact with it. In the following chapters, we further explore the standards for 6–8 that incorporate technology, suggest specific applications and strategies, and provide lessons to help students successfully achieve those standards.

Chapter 8

Practical Ideas for Sixth Grade

We realize that you will want to focus on your particular grade or subject when you are planning your lessons and implementing CCSS, so we have organized the Practical Ideas chapters by grade level, then subject. Each grade starts with an overview followed by ELA technology standards with accompanying apps, software, and websites that you can use to help your students succeed with that standard. We then continue with the math standard for the grade level, also with accompanying resources. Finally, we have included some sample lessons for each grade level in various subject areas. Although we have organized the book so you can find your specific grade and subject easily, please do not disregard other sections of this chapter. It is often helpful to see what the standards require before and after the grade you teach. To see grades other than 6–8, look for our three additional titles in this collection, as they could provide information to help you differentiate for students at all levels of your class.

The CCSS has been set up to encourage cross-curricular work in English Language Arts for Grades 6–8. Many of the same standards are used throughout all three grade levels, making it imperative for all three levels of teachers to work closely together to make sure that a spiral effect takes place. Many schools have block planning so that teachers of the same grade level can plan together; however, you may have to get creative to find time when teachers from all three levels can meet. You will need to discuss with your administrators how to schedule this. These meetings will help ensure that the technology standards embedded in language arts, reading, and writing are addressed without overlapping across classes. Some suggestions are to meet during school or district professional planning days, during the summer (we know many districts that pay for curriculum and unit writing during the summer), staff meetings, or better yet, building time into the schedule at the beginning of the year.

Math is also an area where the technological tools become more varied and complex as students advance. The math standards are meant to be embedded in and a natural part of the units your students will be studying. Choosing the correct mathematical tools will become an important part of your class's learning. There are wonderful new math resources available to help students become proficient in the standards, especially in the area of technology. We list some of our favorites later in this chapter.

We have pulled out the sixth grade standards that include technology for you, and listed them in this chapter so that you have them at your fingertips. Sixth graders are expected to use technology to enhance their literacy skills, such as comparing and contrasting with "live" video, and using digital texts and multimedia to help with reading comprehension. Writing is also important, using the internet to find sources of information, and then using publishing sources to publish their work, in and out of the classroom. Sixth graders are expected to have excellent typing skills, so you will need to make sure that your students are up to speed. An emphasis on finding needed information quickly and efficiently, as well as taking notes and documenting their sources and presenting their findings in a multimedia presentation, will be expected. Using tools such as digital dictionaries and thesauruses, as well as read-along texts, is also emphasized. Technology should also be used to practice math skills, and students will need to use digital math tools, which are available through software programs, apps, or websites.

Reading Literature Resources

RL.6.7 | READING LITERATURE

Compare and contrast the experience of reading a story, drama, or poem to listening to or viewing an **audio, video**, or live version of the text, including contrasting what they "see" and "hear" when reading the text to what they perceive when they listen or watch.

MANY MEDIA FORMATS READ TEXT aloud to kids. Audio books on CD or some ebooks are great sources. Program sites, such as **Follett Shelf (http://tinyurl.com/oux56og)**, TeachingBooks (www.teachingbooks.com), and **TumbleBooks (http://tumblebooks.com)** [must be purchased]) allow you to have access to multiple ebooks that include fiction and nonfiction. You can also check out many ebooks at your local library or purchase them from booksellers, such as Amazon or Barnes & Noble (especially if you have e-readers). There are also some free ebooks out there. The sites **Project Gutenberg (www.gutenberg.org/)**, **FreeReadFeed (www.freereadfeed.com)**, or **FreeBookSifter (www.freebooksifter.com)** can help you find them. Be aware that there are adult titles on these sites, so choose carefully. Also, sites you pay for provide a much better selection.

Another good resource is **ReadWriteThink (www.readwritethink.org)**. This free site allows students to make an online Venn diagram to compare and contrast what they see and hear when reading the text as opposed to what they perceive when they listen or watch.

Reading History Resources

RH.6-8.7 | READING HISTORY

Integrate visual information (e.g., in charts, graphs, photographs, videos, or maps) with other information in print and **digital texts**.

A MULTIMEDIA STORY IS SOME combination of text, still photographs, video clips, audio, graphics, and interactivity presented on a website in a nonlinear format in which the information in each medium is complementary, not redundant. A multimedia presentation integrates visual information with print and digital texts. Following are sites that feature this type of presentation.

MULTIMEDIA WEBSITES

- **CNN (www.cnn.com):** The Cable News Network site is free but includes ads. It has trending news events and access to text, pictures, and video of current events.

- **The Washington Post (www.washingtonpost.com):** This is the official site of the leading newspaper in our capital. There is access to current events in the nation and world. The site is free but does have ads.

- **NPR (www.npr.org):** This site from National Public Radio is government

Practical Ideas for Sixth Grade

sponsored and so is free with no ads. There are links to current stories with media. Students can listen to the most current NPR Hourly Newscast.

- **MSNBC (www.msnbc.com):** Another cable news site from NBC Universal, this free site does contain ads. You can find all the day's national and world news including video, text, and print.

Your students can produce multimedia sites as well. Creating their own website is a wonderful way to fulfill this standard. You can find many programs that allow you to create professional-looking webpages free. The following are just a few choices.

WEBSITES TO CREATE WEBPAGES

- **Weebly (www.weebly.com):** This is an online website creator that is drag-and-drop easy and includes templates. The basics, which include five pages, are free. There is even an app available.

- **Wix (www.wix.com):** This online website creator is also drag-and-drop easy and includes templates. The basics are free. An app version is available.

- **Webs (www.webs.com):** This online website creator allows you to choose a template and then drag and drop elements on to webpages. Basic functionality is free. There is even an app available.

- **Kafafa (www.kafafa.com):** This online website creator also allows you to choose a template and then drag and drop elements on to webpages. A website is $9.99/month for a class.

- **Shutterfly Share Sites (http://tinyurl.com/5wjpu7):** Manage parent communication, post important reminders, receive auto reminders for events and volunteer duties, share class photos and videos from daily activities and field trips—all free. It's private and secure. A free app is also available.

Writing Resources

WHST.6-8.2a	WRITING HISTORY, SCIENCE, AND TECHNICAL SUBJECTS

Introduce a topic clearly, previewing what is to follow; organize ideas, concepts, and information into broader categories as appropriate to achieving purpose; include formatting (e.g., headings), graphics (e.g., charts, tables), and **multimedia** when useful to aiding comprehension.

> **W.6.2a** | WRITING
>
> Introduce a topic, organize ideas, concepts, and information, using strategies such as definition, classification, comparison/contrast, and cause/effect; include formatting (e.g., headings), graphics (e.g., charts, tables), and **multimedia** when useful to aiding comprehension.

USING A MIND-MAPPING PROGRAM is an effective way for students to organize their ideas, concepts, and information. Educators have used several wonderful software programs for mind-mapping for many years; however, there are also free sites out there that do this. There are even templates, such as a Venn diagram that allows students to compare and contrast and show cause and effect. Following are some digital tools you can use to teach note taking and categorizing.

APPS, SOFTWARE, AND WEBSITES FOR MIND-MAPPING

- **Inspiration (http://tinyurl.com/ygharef):** This mind-mapping software program helps students organize their writing. It can be especially helpful for students who are learning to create paragraphs and organize big ideas into their smaller parts. Cost is $40 to $640. **Webspiration (http://tinyurl.com/bmop3nh)** is the web-based version. Cost is $6/month.

- **Popplet (www.popplet.com):** This is a wonderful online organizational tool for student writing. A free app called **Popplet Lite** is also available. It is easy to use, and students can import pictures and text to create web maps.

- **Bubbl.us (www.bubbl.us):** This is a free (with limited use) mind-mapping website for Grades K–12. It can be shared by multiple students at a time and comes with an accompanying app. For more options, purchase a package for $6/month or $59/year. Both come with a 30-day free trial. Site licensing is available. Contact the company for specifics.

- **Mindmeister (www.mindmeister.com/education):** This is a free, basic mind-mapping website for Grades 2–12. Upgrades are available ($18/month for a single user; $30 per user for 6 months). Educational pricing is available for schools and universities ($6 per user for 6 months). All of the upgrades have a free trial period.

- **FreeMind (http://tinyurl.com/5qrd5):** This is a free mind-mapping tool for Grades 2–12. However, FreeMind is written in Java and will run on almost any system with a Java runtime environment. Options for a basic or maximum install are available.

Creating your own Venn diagram and having kids type in it from a word processing document also works. Another option is to create an online Venn diagram using the free web-based program **ReadWriteThink (www.readwritethink.org)**.

In this standard, you are also asked to include charts, tables, and multimedia when aiding comprehension. Using Microsoft **Excel (www.office.com), Apple Numbers for Mac (www.apple.com/mac/numbers/)**, or **Google Sheets (www.google.com/sheets/about/)** is a good way to teach students about charts and graphs. Making their own charts and graphs helps students learn how to interpret and present information.

SOFTWARE AND WEBSITES TO CREATE CHARTS AND GRAPHS

- **The Graph Club 2.0 (http://tinyurl.com/2rx2k8):** This program can really help students visualize how charts and graphs compare, and it's extremely easy to use. The program includes ready-made activities in all subject areas and includes rubrics and sample graphs. District purchasing and volume CDs are available. Contact a representative on the site for specific prices.

- **Gliffy (www.gliffy.com):** Create professional-quality flowcharts, wireframes, diagrams, and more with this tool. It is free for limited use, and upgrades are available for a fee.

- **Create-a-Graph (http://tinyurl.com/c6wz4):** Create bar, line, area, pie, and XY graphs with this free website. It is easy to use, and you can print, save, or email your completed graphs.

- **ClassTools (www.classtools.net):** Create graphs and charts and use many other helpful classroom tools, such as a QR code generator or timeline, with this free website.

Reading Resources

RST.6-8.9	READING SCIENCE AND TECHNICAL SUBJECTS

Compare and contrast the information gained from experiments, **simulations, video, or multimedia sources** with that gained from reading a text on the same topic.

THERE ARE MANY PLACES TO SEE videos about educational topics. It's up to you to sift through them to find what you are looking for and locate reliable sources. The following are some that we would recommend.

EDUCATIONAL VIDEO SITES

- **WatchKnowLearn (www.watchknowlearn.org):** The site has many free educational videos that allow you access to everything from frog dissection simulations to earthquake destruction. It organizes content by age ranges and provides reviews.

- **NeoK12 (www.neok12.com):** There are many science experiments, simulations, and videos on all sorts of topics on this website. It also guarantees that all videos are kid safe, and as an added bonus, it is free.

- **EarthCam (www.earthcam.com):** This interesting site allows you to go to many different sites around the world and view video from a live camera (for example, Times Square or Wrigley Field).

- **iTunesU (http://tinyurl.com/lbjbarh):** As stated on their website, "Choose from more than 750,000 free lectures, videos, books, and other resources on thousands of subjects from Algebra to Zoology." Access it free through iTunes. A free iTunesU app is also available.

- **BrainPOP (www.brainpop.com):** This website has been around for a long time and is still an oldie but goodie, as it gives educational videos on multiple educational topics, in a fun, cartoon format. Price varies based on the subscription you choose.

Using these various sources, it will be easy for students to compare and contrast the information they gathered from videos, simulations, webpages, or textbooks. Gathering information has never been so engaging!

Publishing Resources

W.6.6	WRITING

Use technology, including the internet, to produce and publish writing as well as to interact and collaborate with others; demonstrate sufficient command of keyboarding skills to type a minimum of three pages in a single sitting.

WHST.6-8.6	WRITING HISTORY, SCIENCE, AND TECHNICAL SUBJECTS

Use technology, including the internet, to produce and publish writing and present the relationships between information and ideas clearly and efficiently.

PRODUCING AND PUBLISHING WRITING digitally is another standard sixth graders are expected to meet. There are many websites that allow you to publish student writing. Using blogging websites such as **Edmodo (www.edmodo.com)**, **TeacherBlogIt (www.teacherblogit.com)**, and **Wikispaces (www.wikispaces.com)** is another way to share students' writing in a safe, protected environment. Blogging is also a good way for students to interact and collaborate with others. These sites allow teachers to set themselves up as administrators and add students to various groups. All student writing is secure in these groups.

You can give students assignments asking for short answers where everyone can respond, or you can ask them to write longer assignments on their own. They can then work on assignments and submit privately to you, or post them on the site to share.

There are also sites that ask students to submit their work to be considered for publication on their site. Following are a few options.

PUBLISHING WEBSITES

- **Scholastic Publishing (http://tinyurl.com/plwnn6f):** This free website allows teachers to submit student writing for publication.

- **PBS Kids Writing (www.pbskids.org/writerscontest):** This free site asks for student writing and serves as a nice incentive to get students to do their best writing.

- **Lulu (www.lulu.com) and Lulu Jr (www.lulujr.com):** These sites allow you to create real books and publish them online. Parents can purchase the books as a keepsake. The site is free to use, but a fee is required to publish.

- **TikaTok (www.tikatok.com):** This is another site that allows students to write, create, and publish stories as ebooks or hardcover books. **TikaTok Story Spark** is an app that you can purchase for $3. Classroom price for TikaTok starts at $19 a year.

- **Cast UDL Book Builder (http://bookbuilder.cast.org/):** This is a free site that lets you publish your ebook and see what others have published.

- **Poetry Idea Engine from Scholastic (http://tinyurl.com/nm2gtba):** The site allows students to use templates to make different forms of poetry—another great way technology gets kids writing. Better still, it is free!

Following are some apps that allow students to create shorter versions of their stories in an animated way.

APPS AND WEBSITES USING ANIMATION

- **iFunFace (www.ifunface.com):** Students can create a read-aloud to show how the main idea and details flow by using a photo and audio recording to create an animation. This helps students visualize how to support details that branch off from the main ideas and how they all flow together. The app is free but can be upgraded for $1.99.

- **Blabberize (www.blabberize.com):** Students can speak the text and use photos to illustrate in an animated format. Free.

- **Voki (www.voki.com):** Students can use their voices to speak the text, and photos can be used to illustrate in an animated format. It is free, but there are ads.

- **Fotobabble (www.fotobabble.com):** Students' voices can speak the text, and photos can be used to illustrate. Free.

These are not conducive to stories in paragraph form; however, you can use your voice to speak the text. Photos can be used to illustrate stories in an animated format.

KEYBOARDING SOFTWARE

By sixth grade, students are expected to type three pages in one sitting. There are many keyboarding programs available for purchase. Following are just a few.

- **Mavis Beacon Keyboarding Kidz (http://tinyurl.com/254v9on):** Set words-per-minute goals and discover what keys you need to practice and what keys you know well. Play games to practice what you've learned and to improve your speed and accuracy to become a typing pro. ($19.99)

- **Type to Learn (www.ttl4.sunburst.com):** This typing program for Grades K–12 emphasizes both accuracy and words-per-minute speed. It also provides each student with individualized remediation and goals for success. Consult the website for various pricing options and to request a quote.

- **Typing Training (www.typingtraining.com):** This web-based program with apps for Grades 3–12 allows access from any computer or handheld device. Animated coaches are available with a customizable curriculum. Students can play games or choose from more than 2,500 unique exercises while tracking progress with detailed reports and graphs. Consult the website for various options and to request a quote.

FREE KEYBOARDING SITES

Paying for a good typing program is worth the expense. Quality programs keep track of student progress and levels of proficiency and teach necessary skills. If you can't buy a program, there are many free sites that offer some instruction and games.

- **Dance Mat Typing (www.bbc.co.uk/guides/z3c6tfr):** This free website by BBC Schools teaches typing for younger children.

- **TypingWeb (www.typing.com):** This site has ads, but it does keep track of student progress, and it provides reports for free.

- **TypeRacer (www.play.typeracer.com):** This is a free website that allows you to race opponents by typing words in paragraph form. This is great for experienced typists to bone up on accuracy and typing speed. There are ads.

Some districts have students go to a computer lab to practice keyboarding. Other schools fit it in where they can in the classroom, and still others have students practice and learn at home. The best way is to combine all three. Students benefit from formal keyboarding instruction, even at the sixth grade level, but then they need to practice both in the classroom and at home. When students work at computers in your classroom, remind them to practice good technique, such as sitting up straight, keeping hands in home row, holding wrists slightly curved, and moving fingers instead of the hands.

Information Gathering Resources

RI.6.7 | READING INFORMATION

Integrate information presented in different **media or formats** (e.g., visually, quantitatively) as well as in words to develop a coherent understanding of a topic or issue.

W.6.8 | WRITING

Gather relevant information from multiple print and **digital sources**; assess the credibility of each source; and quote or paraphrase the data and conclusions of others while avoiding plagiarism and providing basic bibliographic information for sources.

BY THE TIME STUDENTS ARE IN SIXTH grade, they should be able to search the internet independently to gather the information on a given topic. Your class will need guidance, of course, so lessons on internet searching are critical, as well as lessons on media literacy. Media literacy is especially crucial because students now need to be able to critique a website before using it—anyone can put up a webpage. As stated by the **W.6.8** standard, students will also need to be able to take notes from these sites, assess the credibility of each source, and quote or paraphrase the data and conclusions of others. They must do this while avoiding plagiarism, and they must provide a list of bibliographic sources. We discuss these techniques in the following paragraphs.

Although students are net-savvy these days, even sixth graders still need assistance with the basics of searching. Various search engines work differently, and each will give you different information. Therefore, your students need to know how to use multiple engines.

Smart searching will help students avoid wasting time. Teaching them to analyze search results will help them find better information and think more critically about information they find on the internet. Following are some basic guidelines for students.

- Choose your search terms carefully. Be precise about what you are looking for, though you should use phrases and not full sentences.

- Adding more words can narrow a search. Use Boolean searches to narrow your topic with quotation marks. There's a big difference between the term "gopher" and "habitats of gophers in North America."

- Use synonyms! If students can't find what they're looking for, have them try keywords that mean the same thing or are related.

- Type "site." Typing "site:" (with the colon) after your keyword and before a URL will tell many search engines to search within a specific website.

- Add a minus sign. Adding a minus sign (a hyphen) immediately before any word, with no space in between, indicates that you don't want that word to appear in your search results. For example, "Saturn-cars" will give you information about the planet, not the automobile.

Note Taking Resources

Tried and true methods for taking notes, paraphrasing, and summarizing information from books can still be used to gather information and take notes on websites. Teaching students to use data sheets, note cards, and KWL (Know, What, Learn) techniques still works. However, there are now ways that technology can help and sometimes make it easier. The **Kentucky Virtual Library (http://tinyurl.com/ptnwz4)** is a great website to use as a resource for some of these techniques. Evernote allows students to take notes and to import a worksheet, document, or picture (including a snapshot of a webpage) and annotate it using tools that they would use with interactive whiteboard software. It lets them highlight words, cut and paste, and add sticky notes. The sticky notes are especially useful to summarize or paraphrase students' notes. Evernote also allows students to use voice recognition and send their annotated sheet to someone else (including the teacher).

Another way to take notes is to use an "add-on" to your internet browser. The free add-on **Diigo (www.diigo.com)** is made for note taking on docs, PDFs, and screenshots. Students can also save sites and documents as resources to take notes on later with annotations and highlighting.

Modeling is essential when you are teaching your students how to glean information from a website. Your interactive whiteboard is a perfect tool for modeling your lesson. Don't have an interactive whiteboard? Use **RealtimeBoard (www.realtimeboard.com)**. It's a free website that allows you to turn an ordinary whiteboard into an interactive one. All you need is a computer and a projector! Using the many tools an interactive whiteboard and its corresponding software have to offer will really help teach your students how to navigate through information posted on the internet. Using note taking tools when gathering information will help your students organize their research.

APPS FOR NOTE TAKING

- **Inspiration (http://tinyurl.com/ygharef):** This mind-mapping program helps students organize their writing. It can be especially helpful for students who are learning to create paragraphs and organize big ideas into smaller parts. Cost is $40 to $640. **Webspiration (http://tinyurl.com/bmop3nh)** is the web-based version. Cost is $6/month.

- **Popplet (www.popplet.com):** This is a wonderful online organizational tool for student writing. A free app called **Popplet Lite** is also available. It is easy to use, and students can import pictures and text to create web maps.

- **Bubble.us (www.bubble.us):** This is a free (with limited use) mind-mapping website for Grades K–12. It can be shared by multiple students at a time and comes with an accompanying app. For more options, purchase a package for $6/month or $59/year. Both come with a 30-day free trial. Site licensing is available. Contact the company for specifics.

- **Mindmeister (www.mindmeister.com/education):** This is a free, basic, mind-mapping website for Grades 2–12. Upgrades are available ($18/month for a single user; $30 per user for 6 months). Educational pricing is available for schools and universities ($6 per user for 6 months). All of the upgrades have a free trial period.

- **FreeMind (http://tinyurl.com/5qrd5):** This is a free mind-mapping tool for Grades 2–12. FreeMind is written in Java and will run on almost any system with a Java runtime environment. Options for a basic or maximum install are available.

- **Evernote (www.evernote.com):** This is a free app that allows you to import a worksheet, document, or picture (including a snapshot of a webpage) and then annotate it using tools that you would use with interactive whiteboard software. It lets you highlight words, cut and paste, and add sticky notes. It also allows you to use voice recognition. You can then send your annotated sheet to someone else.

Of course, students can also use word documents, such as **Microsoft Office, Apple Pages (www.apple.com/mac/pages)**, or **Google Docs (www.google.com/docs/about)**. Some teachers also make digital templates to help students find specific information and to help students organize their notes, with spaces to summarize or paraphrase.

WEBSITES FOR BIBLIOGRAPHIC SOURCES

Sixth graders will also need to provide basic bibliographic information for sources. Making your own template and having the students fill it in using a word processing program works; however, there are websites that are designed to do this.

- **EasyBib (www.easybib.com):** This is a free website and app for ages 5-12 that students can use to generate citations in MLA, APA, and Chicago formats. Just copy and paste or scan a book's barcode.

- **Citation Machine (www.citationmachine.net):** This is another free website you can use to generate citations in MLA, APA, Turabian, and Chicago formats easily. Just copy and paste, and the website does the rest.

- **StyleWizard (www.stylewizard.com):** This free website generates citations in MLA or APA formats easily. It also has a validity checker and offers career guidance.

Speaking and Listening Resources

> **SL.6.2** | SPEAKING AND LISTENING
>
> Interpret information presented in **diverse media and formats** (e.g., visually, quantitatively, and orally) and explain how it contributes to a topic, text, or issue under study.

> **W.6.5** | SPEAKING AND LISTENING
>
> Include **multimedia components (e.g., graphics, images, music, sound)** and visual displays in presentations to clarify information.

MICROSOFT POWERPOINT HAS BEEN THE presentation program of choice; however, there is now a free individual version called **Microsoft Online (www.office.com)** that includes PowerPoint. Although this is still a great program to use, similar presentation programs have emerged. Apple offers **Keynote (www.apple.com/mac/keynote)** free, but the iPad/iPod version does cost. Its features are very similar to PowerPoint. Another program that has emerged is **Google Slides (www.google.com/slides/about/)**. There are other resources that help with presentations, such as **Microsoft Draw (www.office.com)** and Google Drawings (www.google.com/drive). Office is aimed toward business presentations; however, Google

Drive products such as Slides and Drawings are free and web based. Google slides is also very easy to share, and multiple users can work on a document at once, even from home—which makes this an especially useful program for interacting and collaborating with others. Students can also add audio recordings to their slides, as well as visual displays such as pictures and short video clips. You could also have your students use the following digital tools to develop speaking and listening skills.

SOFTWARE, WEBSITES, AND APPS TO CREATE MOVIES AND SLIDESHOWS

- **iMovie (www.apple.com/ios/imovie/):** This app ($4.99), which also comes as a program, has many uses in the classroom. Students can use it to create full edited videos or short 1-minute trailers. The trailers can be very useful for recounting and presenting ideas to others.

- **Animoto (www.animoto.com):** This website allows you to turn your photos and music into stunning video slideshows. Educational use is free for unlimited videos of 20 minutes.

- **MovieMaker (www.moviemaker.com):** The program is Microsoft's version of a movie-editing program. It comes standard with any Windows computer.

- **Prezi (www.prezi.com):** You can sign up for a free educational account, and your students can create and share presentations online. Prezi has mind-mapping, zoom, and motion, and it can import files. Presentations can be downloaded. A Prezi viewer app is available.

- **Wideo (www.wideo.co [.co not .com]):** Wideo allows you to easily make animation videos. Education pricing is $0.75/month.

- **Explain Everything (www.explaineverything.com):** This $2.99 app uses text, video, pictures, and voice to present whatever your students are asked to create. They can illustrate a story or poem or recount information they hear.

- **Stupeflix (https://studio.stupeflix.com/en/):** Make free movies using your photos and videos for up to 20 minutes. It's easy, and a lot of fun!

- **SchoolTube (www.schooltube.com):** This is the best free source for educators for a video-sharing community where students can watch or post videos.

- **YouTube (www.youtube.com):** There are many short, free videos that your students can listen to, including folktales, science, and people reading popular books that are in your classroom. Your students can listen and then ask and answer questions. There is also a free app.

Language Resources

> **L.6.4c** | LANGUAGE
>
> Consult reference materials (e.g., dictionaries, glossaries, thesauruses), both print and **digital**, to find the pronunciation of a word or determine or clarify its precise meaning or its part of speech.

ALTHOUGH DIGITAL DICTIONARIES and thesauruses are not updated as often as digital encyclopedias, they are still very convenient to use and are kept current. These sites should be bookmarked or put on your website for easy access. The more students use them, the more comfortable they will become. You should do lessons and activities to learn and practice the necessary skills with an online dictionary.

DIGITAL DICTIONARY AND THESAURUS WEBSITES

- **Merriam-Webster (www.merriam-webster.com):** This is a free digital dictionary for all ages. It is the most commonly used digital dictionary, and it includes a thesaurus.

- **WordSmyth (www.wordsmyth.net):** This site shows three levels of a student dictionary. When looking up a word, you also see links to a thesaurus and rhyming dictionary for that word. You can sign up for an ad-free version that will not cost your school.

- **Word Central Kids (www.wordcentral.com):** This student online dictionary includes an audio pronunciation of the word as well as the definition. There are many teacher resources.

- **Thesaurus.com (www.thesaurus.com):** This is a fine thesaurus site with many extra features. It does have some ads, but it is available online and as an app.

- **Wordle (www.wordle.net):** This is a free site for generating "word clouds" from text that you provide. The clouds give greater prominence to words that appear more frequently in the source text. You can tweak your clouds with different fonts, layouts, and color schemes.

- **Tagxedo (www.tagxedo.com):** This is a free site that turns the words of famous speeches, news articles, slogans and themes into visually stunning word clouds.

Using the app or website **Trading Cards (http://tinyurl.com/8lqftek)** is a good way to document vocabulary words by adding their definitions and a picture, and recording voices for pronunciation. You can also use Trading Cards by doing an activity with an online thesaurus. You can give a student a word on a trading card, and then ask them to make as many trading cards as they can of synonyms and antonyms of that word. Students can print these out and trade them with others, or make them into a digital book. The app Explain Everything is also easy to use to import a picture, record your voice, and make a digital presentation.

Math Resources

MP5	MATH
Use appropriate **tools** strategically.	

THERE ARE TWO MAIN SETS OF STANDARDS, processes and practices, for the Common Core Math standards. First, you have the math targets, written similarly to ELA (Ratios & Proportional Relationships, The Number System, Expressions & Equations, Geometry, and Statistics & Probability). While you work with sixth grade students on mathematical processes, such as Expressions & Equations or Geometry, you need to teach your students how to apply the Standards for Mathematical Practices (which include problem solving and precision) to those processes. One practice, the only one that includes technology, is mathematical practice 5, "Use appropriate tools strategically."

Following is the explanation CCSS provides for **MP5**. As this is the standard explanation for Grades K–12, it does include references to higher grades.

> Mathematically proficient students consider the available tools when solving a mathematical problem. These tools might include pencil and paper, concrete models, a ruler, a protractor, **a calculator, a spreadsheet, a computer algebra system, a statistical package, or dynamic geometry software**. Proficient students are sufficiently familiar with tools appropriate for their grade or course to make sound decisions about when each of these tools might be helpful, recognizing both the insight to be gained and their limitations. For example, mathematically proficient high school students analyze graphs of functions and solutions generated using a **graphing calculator**. They detect possible errors by strategically using estimation and other mathematical knowledge. When making mathematical models, they know that **technology** can enable them to visualize the results of varying assumptions, explore consequences, and compare predictions with data. Mathematically proficient students at various grade

levels are able to identify relevant external mathematical resources, such as **digital content located on a website**, and use them to pose or solve problems. They are able to use technological tools to explore and deepen their understanding of concepts.

Because this description did not give examples for all grades, we have provided lists of appropriate apps, websites, software, and lessons that will help translate this standard for sixth grade.

Currently, this is the only sixth grade math standard that involves technology. Since using any kind of technology to have students practice math can grab their attention, help long-term learning, and make math fun, technology is a math tool students should use as much as possible. There are many math programs, websites, and apps out there, which allow students to explore and deepen their understanding of math concepts. The best of them have students learning in creative ways and are not just electronic worksheets. They automatically adapt to the students' skill level, and they give you the data you need to know where students are in their learning and what they need to effectively continue. Following are many good math resources. Some are free. Some are not. Unfortunately, the free resources, many with ads, are usually less interesting to your students and are not as well organized. They don't give you the feedback you need. It is up to you to decide what is best for your circumstances and budget.

Following are some websites you can use to help students meet the sixth grade math standards.

MATH WEBSITES

- **ScootPad (www.scootpad.com):** This is a web-based math site that is customizable for individual students. It adapts to the student and keeps the teacher in the loop with multiple reports. It is completely aligned to the CCSS. The price for a class varies from $5 to $20/month.

- **DreamBox Learning Math (www.dreambox.com):** Individualized, adaptive game-based math that keeps kids coming back for more. Available online or through an app. Price is $12.95/month (home) or $25/month (school), less if packaged.

- **Study Island (www.studyisland.com):** This is a web-based program where students work on engaging, interactive lessons and activities at their own pace to learn aligned Common Core math standards. Teachers can also choose to guide students and assign specific areas to work through. This program must be purchased. Pricing information is available on the website.

- **IXL (www.ixl.com/math):** This site features adaptive individualized math through gameplay. It gives students immediate feedback and covers many skills, despite its emphasis on drills. Levels range from pre-kindergarten to eighth grade. There is a limited free version. Class price is $199/year.

- **XtraMath (XtraMath.org):** This is a great site for practicing math facts. It keeps track of student progress, it's easy to pick what you want your students to work on, and it's easy for kids to use independently. It is free; however, you can purchase an extended version.

- **Coolmath-Games (www.coolmath-games.com), SoftSchools (www.softschools. com), Sheppard Software (http://tinyurl.com/ccrxoa), AAA Math (www.aaa-math.com),** and **PBS Kids Cyberchase (http://pbskids.org/cyberchase/)** are several sites that have free math games that cover all math topics at each grade level. However, they have ads, are not able to track students' success rates, and are not generally self-adaptive to students' skill levels.

- **Khan Academy (www.khanacademy.org):** This free website has every math application you can think of and has short video tutorials on how to solve them! The site includes feedback and many resources.

- **AdaptedMind (http://tinyurl.com/997geeg):** This site provides good practice for all sorts of sixth grade mathematical problems.

- **WebQuests (www.webquest.org):** These are great tools to use for presentations. WebQuest is a website that allows students to follow an already-created, project-based lesson where information is found solely on the internet. You can also create your own WebQuest if you have a website-building program or a website like **Kafafa (www.kafafa.com/kafafa)**. WebQuest.org is the original and most popular site, but if you search the internet, you will find more sites that you can use.

RECOMMENDED MATH APPS
- **Math Blaster HyperBlast (http://tinyurl.com/q3ff7vg):** The classic game many teachers used when they were students, now updated. The price is $0.99 to 1.99.

- **Geoboard (http://tinyurl.com/kzyxjv7):** This app is the digital recreation of a geoboard. The app is simple to use, and the geometry activities are open-ended and endless. The app is free.

- **Swipea Tangram Puzzles for Kids (http://tinyurl.com/nsnoazj):** This is a digital version of tangrams where students can manipulate, flip, and rotate shapes to create different pictures. The app is free.

- **Explain Everything (www.explaineverything.com):** This $2.99 app uses text, video, pictures, and voice to present whatever your students are asked to create.

As stated in the standard, "Mathematically proficient students consider the available tools when solving a mathematical problem. These tools might include a calculator, a spreadsheet, a computer algebra system, a statistical package, or dynamic geometry software. Proficient students are sufficiently familiar with tools appropriate for their grade or course to make sound decisions about when each of these tools might be helpful, recognizing both the insight to be gained and their limitations."

Many sites offer math tools, such as a graphing calculator. SoftSchool has an elementary-level graphing calculator. IXL allows you to create your own graph paper that you can then use with an interactive whiteboard if you have one. Use RealtimeBoard if you do not have an interactive whiteboard. Some good programs and sites to use when graphing include Gliffy, Create-a-Graph, and ClassTools.

In sixth grade, students are also expected to use a protractor to measure angles. They can use the app **Protractor 1st (www.skypaw.com/apps/)**, which is part of the Multi Measures 2 app that includes a converter that can measure pairs of units. It can be used just like a regular protractor and is a converter as well. **Softpedia (www.softpedia.com)** is a site that allows you to download a protractor to use online. The site is free, but has ads. Using your interactive whiteboard tool's protractor also works well.

Literacy Lessons

Cross-curriculum planning is encouraged with the Common Core by using ELA standards in history, science, and technical subjects. However, we encourage you to go further and include the arts, math, and physical education teachers in your planning. How will you ever get through everything if you teach standard by standard? The key to planning with the CCSS is by teaching multiple standards in one lesson, when you can. We hope that the following list of a few sample lessons for sixth grade will inspire you to become an effective technology lesson planner.

WORD CLOUDS

The following lesson asks students to create a Wordle or a word cloud. You can use a concept or novel that students are studying to provide a list of words. This could be spelling words, vocabulary words, site words, nouns and verbs, characters, plot, and so on. Students should be encouraged to use resource materials to find as many creative words as they can, which would then satisfy **L.6.4c**. In addition, students should feel free to explore the different formatting tools to make their Wordle or word cloud stand out. Finished projects can be displayed around the classroom, scanned and uploaded to a website, or made into a book. This is fun with a purpose, because students use technology to produce and publish writing. They also interact and collaborate with each other, which satisfies **W.6.6**. And, if you are using this as an activity for stories or plays, it satisfies **SL.6.5** by adding visual displays to emphasize or enhance certain facts or details. Students are developing a coherent understanding of the topic or issue and presenting it in a different media format, so **RI.6.7** is also satisfied.

MOVIE TRAILERS

For this next lesson, you will need to do a little prep before you begin. Start with an internet search for student iMovie Trailer examples. There are some good examples on YouTube. However, you will want to preview these iMovie Trailers before showing them to your students. Begin the lesson with a discussion on the last movie trailers students have seen. Continue the discussion with what makes a good trailer: one that captures the interest of the audience, does not reveal the ending, has music that reflects the mood of the movie, and so on. After viewing several examples, students have a discussion about what made those trailers interesting.

Next, have a discussion about these important elements and how they can be included in a movie trailer:

- Readable text

- Clear recordings

- Interesting, clear images

- Timing of images

- Concise language

- Music that reflects the mood of the book

- Narration that is louder than the background music

- Enough details to be interesting but not enough to give away the ending

- Ends with a question or scene that makes the audience want to read the book

Choose a book you are reading in class, or have students use a self-selected book they are reading independently, because movie trailers make an excellent alternative to book reports. Let the students know your expectations for the completed project. For example:

- Introduce the book: Include the title, the author's name and the genre.

- Tell about the book: Introduce the main characters and action. Don't try to tell every detail.

- Tell about your favorite part of the book or make a connection: Persuade the audience to read the book and leave the audience wanting to know more. For example, explain what the main character has to overcome, but don't tell if he/she is successful.

- Give a recommendation: Provide closure for the book trailer. This also helps match the perfect reader with the book.

- Short and sweet is best.

Using your favorite way to make trailers (iMovie, Animoto, Wideo, etc.), students begin working on the trailers for their book. If students work together collaboratively, **W.6.6** will be satisfied, using technology, including the internet, to produce and publish writing. In the beginning, you may find your students need to plan and organize for their trailer. Apple's iMovie for Mac site has more than 29 free templates to help students work through their trailers. Students may need adult supervision and help when the time comes to scan, upload, or download pictures for their trailer. Certainly students can provide their own illustrations and graphics, either done by hand or digitally using any graphic art program (such as Microsoft Draw or Google Drawings). If their book has pictures, students can scan and use those for their trailers. Or, students can also search the internet to find pictures to use.

Once all trailers are complete, establish a class wiki and post them for everyone to see. You may even wish to publish the address to the class wiki for parents and members of the community to view. Or, trailers can be posted at SchoolTube.

In addition to **W.6.6**, other standards satisfied include **SL.6.5**, as students are using technology to clarify information in their presentations. **SL.6.2** and **RI.6.7** are also satisfied because students are interpreting information using a diverse media format, all to develop a coherent understanding of a topic (their novel or book).

Science/Social Studies Lessons

The following sample lessons address CCSS ELA standards and teach lessons based on national standards in social studies and science.

AROUND THE WORLD

Sixth graders across the country study people, places, and societies from around the world. This lesson was given by a history teacher in conjunction with a technology teacher/coach. Students worked on the project in both of the classes. In this exercise, students describe the influence of individuals and groups on historical and contemporary events within a specific country or region. They identify the location and geographic characteristics of their chosen society, because geography also influences the locations and characteristics of societies. Identifying different ways of organizing economic and government systems for that society is a goal for students. Citizenship should also be discussed. For example, what does it mean to be a member of a society, an educational institution, or a religious institution? Students should also identify and include major physical and human geographic figures such as landforms, bodies of water, and major cities.

Students will use research they gather from multiple print and digital sources (**W.6.8**), (making sure to quote sources accurately as well as citing each one) to put together a photo story presentation on a foreign country they have been assigned or chosen. Each photo must cite the website the picture was obtained from. Each slide needs a narration of key facts. Give students a choice of ways they can display their research (Microsoft PowerPoint, Keynote, iMovie Trailer, Prezi, etc.). Following are some key elements to include in a presentation:

- Name of the country

- Map of the country

- Flag of the country

- One or more major landforms

- One or more famous landmarks

- Type of government

- Type of economic system

- One or more major export

- Official language(s) of country

- Religions of country

- Major holidays celebrated

- Special foods from the country

- Famous person from that country

Since students may be working on this project in several locations, you may want to encourage them to create a Google folder to store photos of their country. Students could use a Google Doc to write their script and record websites as they go along. Another idea is to have students save everything to a zip drive (USB), which they can easily bring back and forth to classes. Final projects will be presented to the class. You may wish to have students digitally take notes during each presentation.

In addition to **W.6.8**, many other standards are satisfied with this lesson. **WHST.6-8.2a**, **WHST.6-8.6**, **SL.6.5**, and **RI.6.7**, as well as **SL.6.2**, are satisfied when students introduce, organize, interpret, and illustrate their information and ideas. **RH.6-8.7** and **W.6.2** will also be satisfied, as students will need to put together a presentation using information they gained, clearly and efficiently to aid comprehension. **W.6.6** and **L.6.4c** are also satisfied, as students are working together to publish a presentation for which they used multiple digital sources.

DISEASES

Science teachers we know used this lesson to teach about disease. One objective teachers had was to tie in reading and writing with science. Teachers first developed a list of diseases in various categories. For example:

- Communicable diseases:

- influenza

- measles

- hepatitis

- mononucleosis

- meningitis

- Ebola

- tuberculosis

- Noncommunicable diseases:

- diabetes

- heart disease

- cancer

- sickle cell anemia

- hypertension

- osteoporosis

- Alzheimer's

Next, teachers found articles, text, movies, and so on, about as many of the diseases as they could. Time was spent reading and discussing diseases, causes, and cures. Students were then allowed to choose a disease to research. Teachers had specific information that needed to be included in each presentation. For example:

1. What causes this disease?

2. What are the symptoms for this disease? (How do people know if they have the disease?)

3. How is the disease spread among humans (if it is)?

4. How can the disease be prevented? If it can't be prevented, explain why not.

5. After a person has the disease, what is the treatment? If there is no treatment available, explain the current research and what is being done to find a treatment or cure.

6. List three important facts about the disease not already mentioned.

7. Cite your sources.

Students next spend time researching their disease using a variety of print and digital sources (**W.6.8**). Give students a choice of ways they can display their research

(Microsoft PowerPoint, Keynote, iMovie Trailer, Prezi, etc.). Once all projects are complete and have been presented to the class, establish a class wiki and post them for everyone to see. You may even wish to publish the address to the class wiki for parents and members of the community to view. Or, projects can be posted at SchoolTube.

In addition to **W.6.8**, many other standards are satisfied with this lesson. **WHST.6-8.2a**, **WHST.6-8.6**, **SL.6.5**, and **RI.6.7**, as well as **SL.6.2**, are satisfied when students introduce, organize, interpret, and illustrate their information and ideas. **RH.6-8.7** and **W.6.2** will also be satisfied, as students will need to put together a presentation using information they gained, clearly and efficiently to aid comprehension. **W.6.6** and **L.6.4c** are also satisfied, as students are working together to publish a presentation where they used multiple digital sources.

Math Lessons

The following lesson samples help students meet the technology benchmarks found in standard **MP5**.

MATHEMATICAL REASONING

In sixth grade, students need to be able to explain their mathematical reasoning to others, as part of the **MP5** standard. Explain Everything is one resource they can use to convey their understanding. Students make their own math videos using this app to explain a concept. An example of this is showing fractions. Students can use a tablet (or other device) and take a picture of something that has equal parts (examples: tiles, cement blocks, door frames, windows). Students are encouraged to find examples of equivalent as well as mixed fractions. Next, they use Explain Everything to show how they would represent a fraction (such as 4 ¾) by drawing and shading 4 whole parts first and then shading in 3 out of the 4 next equal parts. Students are encouraged to upload their fraction pictures to help illustrate their fraction examples. The pencil feature on Explain Everything is useful to draw lines (dividing fractions into pieces) right on the uploaded picture. Different colors for shading can be chosen as well. Add another by shading in 2 out of 3 and adding these fractions together. They can then record their voice explaining their fraction pictures. In addition to math standard **MP5**, many other standards are satisfied with this lesson. **WHST.6-8.2a**, **WHST.6-8.6**, **SL.6.5**, and **RI.6.7**, as well as **SL.6.2**, are satisfied when students introduce, organize, interpret, and illustrate their fraction problem using Explain Everything.

MATH EXPLORATIONS

A local sixth grade class had great fun with the following math exploration, which they adapted from a WebQuest developed at George Mason University. Students work in pairs to plan a three-day trip to New York City with limited time and a limited budget. They need to decide how they will get there, where they will stay, and what they will see and do. Each team must put together a proposal, including cost, which they will share with the class. They also need to put together a presentation that convinces others that their proposal is the best. Resources and websites for this lesson can be found on **our website at http://tinyurl.com/oexfhcv.**

First, students use resources you provide to choose the best way to travel to New York City. They might go by air, train, or bus.

Next students decide where they will stay while in New York City. You may want to suggest to students that since New York is a very large city, they should look for a place to stay in Manhattan, near Times Square. You may also want to mention that there are websites that offer packages for airfare and hotel accommodations (included on our website).

It is important to remind students that they do not need to make an account at any of these travel websites when searching for fares. They can search without logging in.

Next, teams need to decide what they will see and do while in New York. They need to be reminded that with travel, they only have two days for sightseeing.

Finally, students need to decide a budget for their trip. Students may need some background knowledge on how to make a budget. Others may decide their budget after they do their research. You may wish to have a template for students to record their budget, or give them guidelines on how to set up a budget. This budget item analysis sheet would be shared with the class. Give students a choice of ways they can display their research (Microsoft PowerPoint, Keynote, iMovie Trailer, Prezi, etc.). Students next put together a presentation outlining their choices, keeping in mind they need to convince the class their trip is economical and the best!

In addition to math standard **MP5**, many other standards are satisfied with this lesson. **WHST.6-8.2a**, **WHST.6-8.6**, **SL.6.5**, and **RI.6.7**, as well as **SL.6.2**, are satisfied when students introduce, organize, interpret, and illustrate their information and ideas. **RH.6-8.7** and **W.6.2** will also be satisfied, as students will need to put together a presentation using information they gained, clearly and efficiently to aid comprehension. **W.6.6** and **L.6.4c** are also satisfied as students are working together to publish their presentation, where they used multiple digital sources. Students also need to cite their sources in their presentation, which satisfies **W.6.8**.

A Final Note

As students progress through the grades, they are establishing their baseline of proficiency in technology. This will definitely enhance students' experiences with technology in high school, as well as satisfy the CCSS performance standards at the 6–8 level. We hope that you found the resources and lesson ideas presented in this chapter useful and that they are easy to adapt to your class.

You will find more resources online at **our website (http://tinyurl.com/oexfhcv)**, which may be helpful to you as you look to differentiate your instruction. Visit our site for updated information about this book. To learn more about meeting technology standards found within the CCSS for other grades, look for our three additional titles in this collection.

Chapter 9

Practical Ideas for Seventh Grade

We realize that you will want to focus on your particular grade or subject when you are planning your lessons and implementing CCSS, so we have organized the Practical Ideas chapters by grade level and subject. Each grade starts with an overview followed by ELA technology standards with accompanying apps, software, and websites that you can use to help your students succeed with that standard. We then continue with the math standard for the grade level and review appropriate resources. Finally, we have included some sample lessons for each grade level in various subject areas. Although we have organized the book so you can find your specific grade and subject easily, please do not disregard other sections of this chapter. It is often helpful to see what the standards require before and after the grade you teach. To see grades other than 6-8, look for our three additional titles in this collection, as they could provide information to help you differentiate for students at all levels of your class.

The CCSS has been set up to encourage cross-curricular work in English Language Arts from Grades 6-8. Many of the same standards are used throughout all three grade levels, making it imperative for all three levels of teachers to work closely together to make sure that a spiral effect takes place. Many schools have block planning so that teachers of the same grade level can plan together; however, you may have to get creative to find time when teachers from all three levels can meet. You will need to discuss with your administrators how to schedule this. These meetings will help ensure that the technology standards embedded in language arts, reading, and writing are addressed without overlapping across classes. Some suggestions are to meet during school or district professional planning days, during the summer (we know many districts that pay for curriculum and unit writing during the summer), during staff meetings, or better yet, during scheduled times your school builds in at the beginning of the year.

Math is also a subject area where technological tools become more varied and complex as students advance. The math standards are meant to be imbedded in and a natural part of the units your students will be studying. Choosing the correct math tools will become an important part of your class's learning. There are wonderful new math resources available to help students become proficient in the standards, especially in the area of technology. We list some of our favorites later in this chapter.

We have pulled out the seventh grade standards that include technology for you, and listed them in this chapter so that you have them at your fingertips. Seventh graders are expected to use technology to enhance their literacy skills, such as comparing and contrasting a literary work to its audio, filmed, staged or multimedia version. They will be required to use digital texts and multimedia to help with reading comprehension, and to be able to organize information. Writing is also important, using the internet to find sources of information, and then using publishing sources to publish their work, in and out of the classroom. An emphasis on finding needed information quickly and efficiently, as well as taking notes, documenting, linking as well as citing sources, and presenting their findings in a multimedia presentation, will be expected. Using tools such as digital dictionaries and thesauruses, as well as read-along texts, is also emphasized. Technology should also be used to practice math skills, and students will need to use digital mathematical tools, which are available through software programs, apps, or websites.

Literacy Resources

> **RL.7.7** | READING LITERATURE
>
> Compare and contrast a written story, drama, or poem to its **audio, filmed, staged,** or **multimedia** version, analyzing the effects of techniques unique to each medium (e.g., lighting, sound, color, or camera focus and angles in a film).

> **RI.7.7** | READING INFORMATIONAL TEXT
>
> Compare and contrast a text to an **audio, video,** or **multimedia** version of the text, analyzing each medium's portrayal of the subject (e.g., how the delivery of a speech affects the impact of the words).

> **RH.6-8.7** | READING HISTORY
>
> Integrate visual information (e.g., in charts, graphs, photographs, **videos,** or maps) with other information in print and **digital texts.**

Audio Books

There are some free ebooks out there. Using the sites, **Project Gutenberg (www. gutenberg.org/), FreeReadFeed (www.freereadfeed.com)** or **FreeBookSifter (www. freebooksifter.com)** are possibilities. There are adult titles on these sites too. Choose carefully. Though, of course, the sites that you pay for give you a much better selection. You can also check out many ebooks from your local library or purchase them from booksellers such as Barnes & Noble. Following are a few places to find audio books.

WEBSITES FOR AUDIO BOOKS

- **FreeClassicAudioBooks (www.freeclassicaudiobooks.com):** This site houses many classic titles for free download. There are ads.

- **Follett Shelf (http://tinyurl.com/oux56og):** This is one of a group of online providers (must be purchased) that allow you to have access to multiple ebooks, which include fiction as well as nonfiction. Various pricing.

- **TeachingBooks (www.teachingbooks.net):** This is among a group of online providers (must be purchased) that allow you to have access to multiple ebooks, which include fiction as well as nonfiction.

After listening or reading a familiar story or text, then listening to the audio version, students can use a Venn diagram, including **ReadWriteThink (www.readwritethink. org)**. It's a free site that allows you to make an online Venn diagram to compare and contrast the effects of techniques in audio books such as sound and audio visual, and then analyze each medium's portrayal of the subject (e.g., how the delivery of a speech affects the impact of the words).

Film

As **RL7.7** states, seventh grade students will need to compare and contrast a video or multimedia version to a text. Therefore, videos or multimedia on famous books can be used in order to satisfy this standard. Here are some websites that you can use.

- **NeoK12 (www.neok12.com):** This is a website with short stories on video.

- **Netflix (www.netflix.com):** Film adaptations of Jane Austen's books, Shakespeare's plays, and titles such as Because of Winn-Dixie can be found at sites such as this or free at your local library.

Multimedia

What is a multimedia version of a written story? A multimedia story is some combination of text, still photographs, video clips, audio, graphics, and interactivity presented on a website in a nonlinear format in which the information in each medium is complementary, not redundant. Following are a few examples of sites that feature this type of presentation.

- **CNN (www.cnn.com):** The Cable News Network site is free but includes ads. It has trending news events and access to text, pictures and video of current events.

- **The Washington Post (www.washingtonpost.com):** This is the official site of the leading newspaper in our capital. There is access to current events in the nation and world. The site is free but does have ads.

- **NPR (www.npr.org):** This site from the National Public Radio is government sponsored and so is free with no ads. There are links to current stories with media. Students can listen to the most recent NPR Hourly Newscast.

- **MSNBC (www.msnbc.com):** Another cable news site from NBC Universal, this free site does contain ads. You can find all the day's national and world news including video, text, and print.

Your students can produce multimedia sites as well. Creating a personal website is a wonderful way to fulfill these standards. You can find many programs that allow you to create professional-looking webpages free. The following are just a few choices:

- **Weebly (www.weebly.com):** This is an online website creator that is drag-and-drop easy and includes templates. The basics, which include five pages, are free. There is even an app available.

- **Wix (www.wix.com):** This online website creator is also drag-and-drop easy and includes templates. The basics are free. An app is available.

- **Webs (www.webs.com):** This online website creator allows you to choose a template and then drag and drop elements onto webpages. Basic functionality is free, and an app is available.

- **Kafafa (www.kafafa.com):** This is still another online website creator that is drag-and-drop easy and includes templates. The website is $9.99/month for a class.

- **Shutterfly Share Sites (http://tinyurl.com/5wjpu7):** Manage parent communication, post important reminders, receive auto reminders for events and volunteer duties, share class photos and videos from daily activities and field trips—all free. It's private and secure. Free apps are also available.

Informational Text Resources

RST.6-8.9	READING, SCIENCE, AND TECHNICAL SUBJECTS

Compare and contrast the information gained from experiments, **simulations, video,** or **multimedia** sources with that gained from reading a text on the same topic.

THERE ARE NOW SO MANY PLACES where you can go to get videos on a variety of educational topics. Anyone and everyone puts up videos, so it's up to you to sift through them to find what you are looking for from reliable sources.

EDUCATIONAL VIDEO SITES

- **YouTube (www.youtube.com):** There are many short, free videos that your students can watch, including folktales, science, and people reading popular books that are in your classroom. Your students can listen and then ask and answer questions. There is also a free app.

- **WatchKnowLearn (www.watchknowlearn.org):** The site has many free educational videos that allow you access to everything from frog dissection simulations to earthquake destruction. It organizes content by age ranges and provides reviews.

- **NeoK12 (www.neok12.com):** There are many science experiments, simulations, and videos on all sorts of topics on this website. It also guarantees that all videos are kid safe, and as an added bonus, it is free.

- **EarthCam (www.earthcam.com):** This interesting site allows you to go to many different sites around the world and view video from a live camera (for example, Times Square or Wrigley Field).

- **iTunesU (http://tinyurl.com/lbjbarh):** As stated on their website, "Choose from more than 750,000 free lectures, videos, books, and other resources on thousands of subjects from Algebra to Zoology." It is accessed through iTunes. A free iTunesU app is also available.

- **BrainPOP (www.brainpop.com):** This website has been around for a long time and is still an oldie but goodie, as it gives educational videos on multiple educational topics, in a fun, cartoon format. Price varies based on the subscription you choose.

Using these various sources, it will be easy to have students compare and contrast the information they have learned from videos and simulations to information they glean from web pages or textbooks. Gathering information has never been so engaging!

Research Resources

W.7.2a	READING INFORMATIONAL TEXT

Introduce a topic clearly, previewing what is to follow; organize ideas, concepts, and information, using strategies such as definition, classification, comparison/contrast, and cause/effect; include formatting (e.g., headings), graphics (e.g., charts, tables), and **multimedia** when useful to aiding comprehension.

WHST.6-8.2a	WRITING HISTORY, SCIENCE, AND TECHNICAL SUBJECTS

Introduce a topic clearly, previewing what is to follow; organize ideas, concepts, and information into broader categories as appropriate to achieving purpose; include formatting (e.g., headings), graphics (e.g., charts, tables), and multimedia when useful to aiding comprehension.

USING A MIND-MAPPING PROGRAM IS an effective way for students to organize their ideas, concepts and information. Several excellent software programs have been used for mind-mapping for many years. However, there are also free sites out there. There are even templates, such as a Venn diagram that allows students to compare and contrast and show cause and effect. Following are some digital tools you can use to teach note taking and categorizing.

APPS FOR NOTE TAKING

- **Inspiration (http://tinyurl.com/ygharef):** A mind-mapping software program that helps student organize their writing. It can be especially helpful for students who are learning to create paragraphs and organize big ideas into their smaller parts. Price for the software ranges between $40 to $640. Their web-based version is called **Webspiration (http://tinyurl.com/bmop3nh)**. Cost is $6/month.

- **Popplet (www.popplet.com):** A wonderful online organizational tool for student writing. A free app called **Popplet Lite** is also available. It is easy to use, and students can import pictures and text to create web maps.

- **Bubble.us (www.bubble.us):** This is a free (with limited use) mind-mapping website for Grades K–12. It can be shared by multiple students at a time and comes with an app. For more options, purchase a package for $6/month or $59/year. Both come with a 30-day free trial. Site licensing is available. Contact the company for specifics.

- **Mindmeister (www.mindmeister.com/education):** This is a free, basic mind-mapping website for Grades 2–12. Upgrades are available ($18/month for a single user; $30 per user for 6 months). Educational pricing is available for schools and universities ($6 per user for 6 months). All of the upgrades have a free trial period.

- **FreeMind (http://tinyurl.com/5qrd5):** This is a free mind-mapping tool for Grades 2–12. FreeMind is written in Java and will run on almost any system with a Java runtime environment. Options for a basic or maximum install are available.

- **Evernote (www.evernote.com):** This is a free app that allows you to import a worksheet, document, or picture, including a snapshot of a webpage, and then annotate it using tools that you would use with interactive whiteboard software. It lets you highlight words, cut and paste, and add sticky notes. It also allows you to use voice recognition. You can then send your annotated sheet to someone else.

Of course creating your own Venn diagram and having kids type in it from a word processing document also works. You can also create an online Venn diagram using the free web-based program **ReadWriteThink (www.readwritethink.org)**.

In this standard, you are also asked to include charts, tables, and multimedia when aiding comprehension. Using programs like **Microsoft Excel (www.office.com), Apple Numbers (www.apple.com/mac/numbers/),** or **Google Sheets (www.google. com/sheets/about/)** is a good way to teach charts and graphs. Making their own charts and graphs helps students learn how to interpret and present information.

SOFTWARE AND WEBSITES TO CREATE CHARTS AND GRAPHS

- **The Graph Club 2.0 (http://tinyurl.com/2rx2k8):** This program really helps with visualization to see how charts and graphs compare, and it's extremely easy to use. The program includes ready-made activities in all subject areas and includes rubrics and sample graphs. District purchasing and volume CDs are available. Contact a representative on the site for specific prices.

- **Gliffy (www.gliffy.com):** Create professional-quality flowcharts, wireframes, diagrams, and more. It is free for limited use. Upgrades are available for a fee.

- **Create-a-Graph (http://tinyurl.com/c6wz4):** Create bar, line, area, pie, and XY graphs with this free website. It is easy to use, and you can print, save, or email your completed graphs.

- **ClassTools (www.classtools.net):** Create graphs and charts (and use many other helpful classroom tools like a QR code generator or timeline!) with this free website.

Writing Resources

W.7.6	WRITING
Use technology, including the Internet, to produce and publish writing and link to and cite sources as well as to interact and collaborate with others, including linking to and citing sources	

WHST.6-8.6	WRITING HISTORY, SCIENCE, AND TECHNICAL SUBJECTS
Use technology, including the internet, to produce and publish writing, and present the relationships between information and ideas clearly and efficiently.	

PRODUCING AND PUBLISHING WRITING digitally is another standard seventh graders are expected to meet. There are many websites that allow you to publish student writing. Using blogging websites such as **Edmodo (www.edmodo. com), TeacherBlogIt (www.teacherblogit.com)**, and **Wikispaces (www.wikispaces. com)** lets you share students' writing in a safe, protected environment and is a great way to interact and collaborate with others. These sites allow teachers to set themselves up as administrators and add students to various groups. All of the students' writing is kept secure in these groups.

You can give students assignments asking for short answers where everyone can respond, or you can ask them to write longer assignments on their own. They can then work on assignments and submit privately to you, or post them on the site to share. This is also a good way to interact and collaborate with others, either in school or at home. **Google Docs (www.google.com/docs/about/)** is a great site to use, as it allows students to work on a document or presentation simultaneously at school or at home to promote collaboration.

There are also sites that ask students to submit their work for possible publication on the site.

PUBLISHING WEBSITES

- **Scholastic Publishing (http://tinyurl.com/plwnn6f):** A free website where teachers can submit student writing for publication.

- **PBS Kids Writing (pbskids.org/writerscontest/):** This free site asks for student writing and serves as a nice incentive to get students to do their best writing.

- **Lulu (Lulu.com)** and **Lulu Jr (www.lulujr.com):** These sites allow you to create real books and publish them online. Parents can purchase the books as a keepsake. The site is free to use, but a fee is required to publish.

- **Cast UDL Book Builder (http://bookbuilder.cast.org/):** This free site lets you publish your ebook and see what others have published.

- **Poetry Idea Engine from Scholastic (http://tinyurl.com/nm2gtba):** This site allows students to use templates to make different forms of poetry—another great way technology gets kids writing. Better still, it is free!

Following are some apps that allow students to create shorter versions of their stories in an animated way.

APPS AND WEBSITES USING ANIMATION

- **iFunFace (www.ifunface.com):** Students can create a read-aloud to show how the main idea and details flow by using a photo and audio recording to create an animation. This helps students visualize how to support details that branch off from the main ideas and how they all flow together. The app is free but can be upgraded for $1.99.

- **Blabberize (www.blabberize.com):** Students can speak the text and use photos to illustrate it in an animated format. Free.

- **Voki (www.voki.com):** Students can use their voices to speak the text, and photos can be used to illustrate in an animated format. It is free, but there are ads.

• **Fotobabble (www.fotobabble.com):** Students' voices can speak the text, and photos can be used to illustrate. Free.

These are not conducive to stories in paragraph form; however, you can use your voice to speak the text and photos can be used to illustrate in an animated format.

WEBSITES FOR BIBLIOGRAPHIC SOURCES

Seventh graders will also need to cite their sources. Of course, making your own template and having the students fill it in using a word processing program works; however, there are some websites that can be used.

• **EasyBib (www.easybib.com):** A free website and app for ages 5–12. Students can use this site to generate citations in MLA, APA, and Chicago formats easily. Just copy and paste or scan the book's barcode.

• **Citation Machine (www.citationmachine.net):** This free website can be used to generate citations in MLA, APA, Turabian, and Chicago formats easily. Just copy and paste, and the website does the rest.

• **StyleWizard (www.StyleWizard.com):** Free website you can use to generate citations in MLA, or APA formats easily. Also has a validity checker and career guidance.

Note Taking Resources

W.7.8	WRITING *and*
WHST.6-8.8	WRITING HISTORY, SCIENCE, AND TECHNICAL SUBJECTS

Gather relevant information from multiple print and **digital sources**, using search terms effectively; assess the credibility and accuracy of each source; and quote or paraphrase the data and conclusions of others while avoiding plagiarism and following a standard format for citation.

BY THE TIME STUDENTS ARE IN seventh grade, they should be able to search the internet independently to gather the information that they need on a given topic. Your class may need some reminders on effective searching, so lessons on internet searching are critical, as well as lessons on media literacy. Media literacy is especially crucial, as students now need to be able to critique a website before using it—anyone can put up a webpage. They will also need to be able to assess the credibility and accuracy of each source, and quote or paraphrase the data and conclusions of others while avoiding plagiarism. We discuss these techniques in the following paragraphs.

Although students are sufficiently net savvy these days, even seventh graders still need assistance with the basics of searching. Various search engines work differently, and each will return different information. Therefore, your students need to know how to use multiple engines.

Smart searching will help avoid a lot of wasted time. Teaching students to analyze search results will definitely help them find better information and think more critically about any information they find on the internet. Following are a few guidelines to share with your students.

- Choose your search terms carefully. Be precise about what you are looking for, though you should use phrases and not full sentences.

- Adding more words can narrow a search. Use Boolean searches to narrow your topic with quotation marks. There's a big difference between "gopher" and "Habitats of gophers in North America."

- Use synonyms! If kids can't find what they're looking for, have them try keywords that mean the same thing or are related.

- Type "site." Typing site: (with the colon) after your keyword and before a URL will tell many search engines to search within a specific website.

- Add a minus sign. Adding a minus sign (a hyphen) immediately before any word, with no space in between, indicates that you don't want that word to appear in your search results. For example, "Saturn -cars" will give you information about the planet, not the automobile.

Using tried and true methods for paraphrasing and summarizing information from books can still be used to gather information and take notes on websites. Teaching students to use data sheets, note cards, and KWL (Know, What, Learn) techniques still works. However, there are now ways that technology can help and sometimes make it easier. The **Kentucky Virtual Library (http://tinyurl.com/ptnwz4)** is a great website to use as a resource for some of these techniques. Evernote is a wonderful app that allows students to take notes and to import a worksheet, document, or picture, including a snapshot of a webpage, then annotate it using tools that you would use with interactive whiteboard software. It lets them highlight words, cut and paste, and add sticky notes. The sticky notes are especially useful to summarize or paraphrase students' notes. It also allows them to use voice recognition. They can then send their annotated sheet to someone else (including the teacher).

Another way to take notes is using an "add-on" for your internet browser. The free add-on **Diigo (www.diigo.com)** is made for note taking on docs, pdfs, and screenshots. Students can also save found sites and documents as resources to take notes on later with annotations and highlighting.

Modeling is, of course, essential when you are teaching your students how to glean information from a website. Your interactive whiteboard is a perfect tool for modeling your lesson. Don't have an interactive whiteboard? Use **RealtimeBoard (www.realtimeboard.com)**: It's a free website that allows you to turn an ordinary whiteboard into an interactive one. All you need is a computer and a projector! Using the many tools an interactive whiteboard and software have to offer will really help teach your students how to navigate through information posted on the internet.

Seventh graders will also need to provide basic bibliographic information and cite their sources. Of course, making your own template and having the students fill it in using a word processing program works; however, there are some websites that can be used like EasyBib, Citation Machine, and StyleWizard.

Speaking and Listening Resources

SL.7.2 | SPEAKING AND LISTENING

Analyze the main ideas and supporting details presented in **diverse media and formats** (e.g., visually, quantitatively, and orally) and explain how the ideas clarify a topic, text, or issue under study.

SL.7.5 | SPEAKING AND LISTENING

Include **multimedia components and visual displays** in presentations to clarify claims and findings and emphasize salient points.

TRADITIONALLY, MICROSOFT POWERPOINT HAS been the presentation program of choice, but it can be expensive. There is now a free individual version called **Microsoft Online (www.office.com)** that includes PowerPoint. Although this is still a great program to use, other, similar presentation programs have emerged. Apple offers **Keynote (www.apple.com/mac/keynote/)**, which costs $14.99, but the iPad/iPod version is only $4.99. Its features are very similar to PowerPoint. Another program that has emerged is **Google Slides (www.google.com/slides/about/)**, a free program. There are other resources that help with presentations, such as Microsoft Draw and **Google Drawings (www.google.com/drive)**. Office is aimed toward business presentations; however, Google Drive products like Slides and Drawings are free and web based. Slides is also very easy to share, and multiple users can work on it at once, even from home—which makes this an especially good program to use when interacting and collaborating with others. Students can also add audio recordings to their slides, as well as visual displays such as pictures and short video clips. You could also have your students use the following digital tools.

WEBSITES TO CREATE MOVIES AND SLIDESHOWS

- **iMovie (www.apple.com/ios/imovie/):** This app ($4.99), which also comes as a program, has many uses in the classroom to create full edited videos or short 1-minute trailers. The trailers can be very useful for recounting and presenting ideas to others.

- **Animoto (www.animoto.com):** This website allows you to turn your photos and music into stunning video slideshows. Educational use is free for unlimited videos of 20 minutes.

- **MovieMaker (www.moviemaker.com):** This is Microsoft's version of iMovie. It comes standard with any Windows computer.

- **Prezi (www.prezi.com):** You can sign up for a free educational account, and your students can create and share presentations online. Prezi has mind-mapping, zoom, and motion, and it can import files. Presentations can be downloaded. A Prezi viewer app is available.

- **Wideo (www.wideo.co [.co not .com]):** Wideo allows you to easily make animation videos. Education pricing is $0.75/month.

- **Explain Everything (www.explaineverything.com):** This $2.99 app uses text, video, pictures, and voice to present whatever your students are asked to create. They can illustrate a story or poem or recount information they hear.

- **Stupeflix (https://studio.stupeflix.com/en/):** Make free movies using your photos and videos for up to 20 minutes. It's easy, and a lot of fun!

- **SchoolTube (SchoolTube.com):** This is the best free source for educators for a video-sharing community where students can watch or post videos.

Language Resources

> **L.7.4c** | LANGUAGE
>
> Consult general and specialized reference materials (e.g., dictionaries, glossaries, thesauruses), both print and **digital**, to find the pronunciation of a word or determine or clarify its precise meaning or its part of speech.

WHILE DIGITAL DICTIONARIES and thesauruses are not updated as often as digital encyclopedias, they are still very convenient to use and are kept current. These sites should be bookmarked or put on your website for easy access. The more students use them, the more comfortable they will become. You should do lessons and activities to learn and practice the necessary skills with an online dictionary.

DIGITAL DICTIONARY AND THESAURUS WEBSITES

- **Merriam-Webster (www.merriam-webster.com):** A free digital dictionary for all ages. It is the most commonly used digital dictionary and includes a thesaurus.

- **WordSmyth (www.wordsmyth.net):** This site shows three levels of a student dictionary. When looking up a word, you also see also links to a thesaurus and rhyming dictionary for that word. You can sign up for an ad-free version, which will not cost your school.

- **Word Central (www.wordcentral.com):** A student online dictionary that includes an audio pronunciation of the word as well as the definition. There are many teacher resources.

- **Thesaurus.com (www.thesaurus.com):** This is a fine thesaurus site with many extra features. It does have some ads, but it is available online and as an app. The site is free.

Using the app or website **Trading Cards (http://tinyurl.com/8lqftek)** is a good way to document vocabulary words by adding their definitions and a picture, and recording voices for pronunciation. You can also use Trading Cards by doing an activity with an online thesaurus. You can give a student a word on a trading card, and then ask them to make as many trading cards as they can of synonyms and antonyms of that word. Students can print these out and trade them with others, or make them into a digital book. The app Explain Everything is also easy to use to import a picture, record your voice, and make a digital presentation.

Math Resources

MP5	MATH

Use appropriate **tools** strategically.

THERE ARE TWO MAIN SETS OF standards, processes and practices, for the Common Core Math standards. First, you have the math targets, written similarly to ELA (Ratios & Proportional Relationships, The Number System, Expressions & Equations, Geometry, and Statistics & Probability). While you work with seventh grade students on mathematical processes, such as Expressions & Equations or Geometry, you need to teach your students how to apply the Standards for Mathematical Practices (which include problem solving and precision) to those processes. One practice, the only one that includes technology, is mathematical practice 5, "Use appropriate tools strategically."

Following is the explanation CCSS provides for **MP5**. As this is the standard explanation for Grades K–12, it does include references to higher grades.

> Mathematically proficient students consider the available tools when solving a mathematical problem. These tools might include pencil and paper, concrete models, a ruler, a protractor, **a calculator, a spreadsheet, a computer algebra system, a statistical package, or dynamic geometry software**. Proficient students are sufficiently familiar with tools appropriate for their grade or course to make sound decisions about when each of these tools might be helpful, recognizing both the insight to be gained and their limitations. For example, mathematically proficient high school students analyze graphs of functions and solutions generated using a **graphing calculator**. They detect possible errors by strategically using estimation and other mathematical knowledge. When making mathematical models, they know that **technology** can enable them to visualize the results of varying assumptions, explore consequences, and compare predictions with data. Mathematically proficient students at various grade levels are able to identify relevant external mathematical resources, such as **digital content located on a website**, and use them to pose or solve problems. They are able to use technological tools to explore and deepen their understanding of concepts.

Because this description did not give examples for all grades, we have provided lists of appropriate apps, websites, software, and lessons that will help translate this standard for seventh grade.

Currently, this is the only seventh grade math standard that involves technology. Since using any kind of technology to have students practice math can grab their attention, help long-term learning, and make math fun, technology is a math tool students should use as much as possible. There are many math programs, websites, and apps out there, which allow students to explore and deepen their understanding of math concepts. The best of them have students learning in creative ways and are not just electronic worksheets. They automatically adapt to the students' skill level, and they give you the data you need to know where students are in their learning and what they need to effectively continue. Following are many good math resources. Some are free. Some are not. Unfortunately, the free resources, many with ads, are usually less interesting to your students and are not as well organized. They don't give you the feedback you need. It is up to you to decide what is best for your circumstances and budget.

Following are some resources we recommend that you can use to enhance the seventh grade math standards.

MATH WEBSITES AND APPS

- **ScootPad (www.scootpad.com):** This is a web-based math site that is customizable for individual students. It adapts to the student and keeps the teacher in the loop with multiple reports. It is completely aligned to the CCSS. The price for a class varies from $5 to $20/month.

- **DreamBox Learning Math (www.dreambox.com):** Individualized, adaptive game-based math that keeps kids coming back for more. Available online or through an app. Price is $12.95/month (home) or $25/month (school), less if packaged.

- **Study Island (www.studyisland.com):** This is a web-based program where students work on engaging, interactive lessons and activities at their own pace to learn aligned Common Core math standards. Teachers can also choose to guide students and assign specific areas to work through. This program must be purchased. Pricing information is available on the website.

- **Explain Everything (www.explaineverything.com):** This $2.99 app uses text, video, pictures, and voice to present whatever your students are asked to create. In seventh grade, students need to be able to explain their mathematical reasoning to others, and this app is a great one to use for this standard. Kids can make their own math videos using this app to explain a concept. They can then record their voice to explain what they did. Other apps such as **Show Me (http://www.showme.com/)** can also be used in this way.

- **IXL (www.ixl.com/math/):** This online site features adaptive individualized math through gameplay. It gives students immediate feedback and covers many skills, despite its emphasis on drills. Levels range from pre-kindergarten to eighth grade. There is a limited free version. Class price is $199/year.

- **XtraMath (www.xtramath.org):** This is a great site for practicing math facts. It keeps track of student progress, it's easy to pick what you want your students to work on, and it's easy for kids to use independently. It is free; however, you can purchase an extended version.

- **Coolmath-Games (www.coolmath-games.com), SoftSchools (www.softschools. com), Sheppard Software (http://tinyurl.com/ccrxoa), AAA Math (www.aaa-math.com),** and **PBS Kids Cyberchase (http://pbskids.org/cyberchase/)** are several sites that have free math games that cover all math topics at each grade level. However, they have ads, are not able to keep track of a student's success rate, and are not generally self-adaptive to the student's own skill level.

- **Khan Academy (www.khanacademy.org):** This free website has every math application you can think of and has short video tutorials on how to solve them! The site includes feedback and many resources.

- **AdaptedMind (http://tinyurl.com/997geeg):** This site provides good practice for all sorts of seventh grade mathematical problems.

- **WebQuests (www.webquest.org):** These are great tools to use for presentations. WebQuest is a website that allows students to follow an already-created, project-based lesson where information is found solely on the internet. You can also create your own WebQuest if you have a website building program or a website like **Kafafa (www.kafafa.com/kafafa)**. WebQuest.org is the original and most popular site, but if you search the internet, you will find more sites that you can use.

MATH APPS
- **Math Blaster HyperBlast (http://tinyurl.com/q3ff7vg):** The classic game many teachers used when they were students, now updated. The price is $0.99 to 1.99.

- **Geoboard (http://tinyurl.com/kzyxjv7):** This app is the digital recreation of a geoboard. The app is simple to use, and the geometry activities are open-ended and endless. The app is free.

- **Swipea Tangram Puzzles for Kids (http://tinyurl.com/nsnoazj):** This is a digital version of tangrams where students can manipulate, flip, and rotate shapes to create different pictures. The app is free.

As stated in the standard, "Mathematically proficient students consider the available tools when solving a mathematical problem. These tools might include a calculator, a spreadsheet, a computer algebra system, a statistical package, or dynamic geometry software. Proficient students are sufficiently familiar with tools appropriate for their grade or course to make sound decisions about when each of these tools might be helpful, recognizing both the insight to be gained and their limitations."

Many sites allow you to use mathematical tools, such as a graphing calculator, or you can use software that comes with your interactive whiteboard—these have all sorts of mathematical tools such as protractors, rulers, and grids. SoftSchool has an elementary-level graphing calculator. IXL allows you to create your own graph paper, which you can then use with your interactive whiteboard. Don't have an interactive whiteboard? Remember to use RealtimeBoard! It's a free website, which allows you to turn an ordinary whiteboard into an interactive one. All you need is a computer and a projector!).

Gliffy, Create-a-Graph, and ClassTools are free sites you can use to make graphs and charts.

In seventh grade, students are also expected to use a protractor to measure angles. They can use the app **Protractor 1st (www.skypaw.com/apps/)**, which is part of the Multi Measures 2 app that includes a converter that can measure pairs of units. It can be used just like a regular protractor and is a converter as well. **Softpedia (www.softpedia.com)** is a site that allows you to download a protractor to use online. The site is free, but has ads. Using your interactive whiteboard tools protractor also works well.

Literacy Lessons

Cross-curriculum planning is encouraged with the Common Core by using ELA standards in history, science, and technical subjects. However, we encourage you to go further and include the arts, math, and physical education teachers in your planning. How will you ever get through everything if you teach standard by standard? The key to planning with the CCSS is to teach multiple standards in one lesson, when you can. We hope that the following list of a few sample lessons for seventh grade will inspire you to become an effective technology lesson planner.

PROJECT BASED LEARNING

At a local middle school, the ELA teacher, tech coach, and librarian collaborated on a project-based learning experience, connecting a literature unit (Under the Persimmon Tree, by Suzanne Fisher Staples) with technology. Students created websites or documentary movies based on the essential question: How does conflict impact people and places? In class, the ELA teacher led students through the reading of the book, having them annotate places of conflict from the book using Evernote. The librarian instructed students in research skills, including using print materials, evaluating online resources, selecting and searching databases, note taking, organizing research, and citing sources. The technology coach/teacher helped students scan or find illustrations for their project and also worked on web page design, as well as how to make a documentary movie. All teachers collaboratively coached students throughout the project, also concentrating on how to write and answer essential questions. Students were also introduced to several web-based tools that they could use during the research process (Evernote, Diigo, etc.), as well as tools for creating websites (Weebly, Wix, Webs, Kafafa and even Shutterfly) and documentaries (iMovie, Animoto, Windows Live Movie Maker, YouTube, Final Cut Pro, etc.). You could have students share their creations with the class. Websites and documentary movies can also be made available for parents to view, as discussed in the writing section above. This project-based learning experience incorporates a multitude of standards. **RH.6-8.7** is satisfied, as students integrate visual information. **WHST.6-8.2a**, **W.7.2a**, **W.7.6**, and **WHST.6-8.6** are also met when students introduce and work their way through the essential question and produce and publish writing, as well as present their ideas clearly and efficiently. **RI.7.7** and **W.7.8** are also satisfied when students gather, integrate, and present their information, in an original way. Using diverse media and formats (including music, graphics, voice-overs, etc.) to present and clarify information is definitely a part of this project, so **SL.7.2** and **SL.7.5** are fulfilled. **L.7.4c**, using reference materials to help with writing, is also satisfied.

TECHNOLOGY COLLABORATION

Another lesson from the files of our middle school friends is a collaboration between the librarian and technology teacher. Picture students wandering the stacks of the library with handheld devices, smartphones, tablets, or anything with a QR reader, excitedly engaged, trying to find that special title, the one they heard others discussing. That book with the code on the back that takes them to a book trailer . . . made by their best friend! This appealing project begins with pairs of students reflecting, planning, and creating their trailer for a book they recommend others read. Using iMovie as the creation app of the trailer, students get at the heart of the conflict and theme of the book in about a minute. A template for each theme helps students plan their words and images before creating their trailer. Next, completed projects are uploaded to the teacher's YouTube channel (the teacher, tech coach, or librarian helps with this step). Finished trailers are also shared with the librarian, who can create, print, and affix a QR code to the back of titles. Books are returned to the stacks with their special codes. The rest is word of mouth! Students share their own projects while promoting books to read with the entire school. This creative and unique way to promote literacy and technology standards includes **RH.6-8.7**, as students must integrate visual information in their iMovie trailer. **WHST.6-8.2a**, **W.7.2a**, **W.7.6**, and **WHST.6-8.6** are also satisfied, as students reflect, plan, create, and publish their trailer, clearly and efficiently. **RI.7.7** and W.7.8 are also met, as students are gathering, integrating, and presenting their information, in an original way (iMovie trailer through a QR code). This project has students definitely using diverse media and formats (including music, graphics, voice-overs, etc.) to present and clarify information. Therefore, **SL.7.2** and **SL.7.5** are satisfied. Last, students are using reference materials to help with writing, so **L.7.4c** is also satisfied.

Social Studies/Science Lessons

The following sample lessons address CCSS ELA standards and teach lessons based on national standards in social studies and science.

HUMAN BODY

Students at this level across the country study the human body. After teaching all of the body systems, our colleagues were looking not only for a unique way for students to show what they learned about a specific human body system, but also an interesting way for them to present to the class. In this lesson, after all teaching and learning is complete, students pick which of the eleven systems they wish to present to the class. Using the app Explain Everything, students draw, appropriately color, and label the entire system. Using their notes, as well as any additional research they found, students record a narration of how their system works. Next, students must present their system to the class. This is done by projecting the tablet with the Explain Everything app onto the interactive whiteboard. Each student listens carefully to each presentation and asks questions at the end. Students giving the presentation must be able to answer the questions quickly and efficiently. Researching and reading about the human body satisfies standard **RI.7.7**. **W.7.2**, **W.7.6**, and **W.7.8** also are addressed with this activity. In addition, the presentation part of this activity satisfies **SL.7.2** and **SL.7.5**.

ANTIQUES ROAD SHOW

Yet another lesson from our middle school friends involves the seventh grade social studies unit on medieval China and Japan during the time when traveling minstrels entertained with their stories. This project was designed so students become modern-day storytellers and animators of historical tales. Students start out reading Beowulf, Adam of the Road, Sign of the Chrysanthemum, or any other book of your choosing that covers that time period. Every year this school traditionally has an author visit. (Coincidentally, the visit was scheduled before this project began. The author stressed to the students how important it is to keep your audience in mind at all times, as well as to research and really know your topic.) Using primary sources, students research the culture of medieval China or Japan through an ancient art piece. Based on that research, students write an "Antiques Roadshow" script, using Microsoft Office, Google, or any word processing tool of your choosing. Next, students need to create a replica of the art (Microsoft, Google Drawings, or any other drawing tool will work). Finally, students are required to video their "Antiques Roadshow" performance (iMovie, Animoto, Windows Live Movie Maker, YouTube, Final Cut Pro, etc.). Puppet pals, iFunFace, Blabberize, Voki, or Fotobabble are also sites students can use for avatars or animation. Students need to be reminded that their presentation needs to be in costumes and scenery that is correct for the time period they researched. You may want to give students a graphic organizer to keep them on track, outlining goals and objectives. Have students share their creations with the class. Finished projects can also be made available for parents to view. This project-based learning experience incorporates many standards. **RH.6-8.7** is satisfied, as students integrate visual information. **WHST.6-8.2a**, **W.7.2a**, **W.7.6**, and **WHST.6-8.6** are also met when students introduce, produce, and publish writing, as well as work together to present their ideas clearly and efficiently. **RI.7.7** and **W.7.8** are also satisfied when students gather, integrate, and present their information in an original way. Using diverse media and formats (including music, graphics, voice-overs, etc.) to present and clarify information is definitely a part of this project, so **SL.7.2** and **SL.7.5** are fulfilled. **L.7.4c**, using reference materials to help with writing, is also satisfied.

Math Lessons

The following two sample lessons satisfy the math practice standard **MP5**.

LOS ANGELES TRIP

A local seventh grade class in our former district had great fun with this math WebQuest, which they adapted from a Kansas middle school WebQuest. Make your own, or do a Google search for math WebQuests to see what is out there! Students plan a five-day trip to Los Angeles, calculating costs and the things that they will do.

After students complete this activity, they will have a good idea of all of the different entertainment and sites to see in LA, as well as the costs of such experiences. Upon completion, students will share their itinerary with the class, explaining how they decided what to do and what not to do. Students will work with a partner, thus satisfying **W.7.6**. Partners decide which section of websites to take, deciding what part (or all) to include in the vacation. For the theater section, students need to include show times that work in the vacation schedule and ticket prices of each show for the number of people who will be attending. Also, students researching the theater section of the vacation will need to read about each show and write a two- to three-sentence summary describing what it is about. This review of each show should be included in the final presentation.

Another partner decides what sights to see and when. Look on each website to find times of tours and other things that the site provides and decide what time works best. Keep track of the ticket prices for each person who will be attending. Write a two- to three-sentence summary of each place, which also needs to be included in your final presentation to the class.

Partners together will decide where to eat. Students can assume that their hotel will provide a free breakfast, but for other meals, a plan needs to be made for eating out. When looking at restaurants, students should compare pricing and decide when to go to each restaurant. Also, students need to figure out what a typical price for dinner will be at the restaurants, including dessert. If students are going to a show after dinner, special attention needs to be paid to the timing of the meal.

Finally, students will need to decide on the most important part of the trip: where to stay. Partners should research hotels in the Los Angeles area and find the one that best meets the needs of their group. They should be reminded not to choose the first one, but instead, compare pricing and keep track of how much the hotel will cost per night. Remember to remind students not to sign up or give any information on any site. Most sites offer free searches.

See **our website** for suggested links to theaters, sights to see, restaurants, and lodging in L.A. as well as other resources your students can use for this activity **(http://tinyurl.com/oexfhcv)**.

When students finish their research, they will share their findings with their partner and discuss what options are the best. Partners should decide together which places and activities they will go to, based on the information they found, and have a rationale for what they chose. Narrow down options if needed. Allow students time to adjust their schedule, change plans, and perhaps even go back to do more research. Once selections have been made and times of events scheduled, partners will need to put the itinerary and presentation together, using Prezi, PowerPoint, or any presentation app or site of choice. Finally, students should present their findings to the class, as well as field any questions and/or suggestions from their classmates and defend their choices. Presentations can also be made available to parents, using some of the sites mentioned earlier. The rubric found in our website (http://tinyurl.com/oexfhcv) is a helpful way to evaluate the quality of your students' work. Our website also has additional resources for this activity.

This project-based learning experience incorporates a myriad of standards. **MP.5** and **RH.6-8.7** are satisfied, as students integrate visual information into their presentations (graphics and even music). **WHST.6-8.2a**, **W.7.2a**, **W.7.6**, and **WHST.6-8.6** are also met when students introduce, produce and publish writing, as well as work together to present their ideas clearly and efficiently. **RI.7.7** and **W.7.8** are also satisfied when students gather, integrate, and present their information, in an original way. Using diverse media and formats (including music, graphics, voice-overs, etc.) to present and clarify information is definitely a part of this project, so **SL.7.2** and **SL.7.5** are fulfilled. **L.7.4c**, using reference materials to help with writing, is also satisfied.

MATH REVIEW

This math lesson, again from the files of one of our middle school friends, is used as a review at the end of a semester, but you could use it to review at the end of any unit. On the whiteboard, the teacher and students made a list of all the concepts and skills studied throughout the semester. In pairs or groups of three (depending how many total), students pick a topic they want to "be an expert" on. Teams next pick the technology method they prefer to present their topic (see our suggestions earlier in **SL.7.2** and **SL.7.5**, or ask students to brainstorm with you) by making a presentation (Prezi), movie (iMovie), Trading Cards, or Explain Everything. When teams finish their presentations, have them project the presentations and "teach" the class. Since this could potentially be before finals, have students take notes for studying, using Evernote, Diigo, or Explain Everything (which can be written and voice recorded), etc. Teams present and project (RealtimeBoard) to the class, making sure they save time for answering any questions, as they are "the experts" on the math topic. These review presentations can then be uploaded to YouTube or any other way you may have to share with absent students and/or parents! They could then be used to review later, or could be great for "flipping the classroom" use. In addition to **MP5**, standard **RH.6-8.7** is satisfied, as students should be encouraged to include visual information into their presentations (graphics and even music). Students are introducing, producing, and publishing writing, as well as working together to present their ideas clearly and efficiently, so **WHST.6-8.2a**, **W.7.2a**, **W.7.6**, and **WHST.6-8.6** are also met. **RI.7.7** and **W.7.8** are also satisfied when students gather, integrate, and present their information, in an original way. Using diverse media and formats (including music, graphics, voice-overs, etc.) to present and clarify information is definitely a part of this project, so **SL.7.2** and **SL.7.5** are also fulfilled.

A Final Note

As students progress through the grades, they are establishing their baseline of proficiency in technology. This will definitely enhance students' experiences with technology in high school, as well as satisfy the CCSS performance standards at the 6–8 level. We hope that you found the resources and lesson ideas presented in this chapter useful and that they are easy to adapt to your class.

You will find more resources online at **our website (http://tinyurl.com/oexfhcv)**, which may be helpful to you as you look to differentiate your instruction. Visit our website for updated information about this book. To learn more about meeting technology standards found within the CCSS for other grades, look for our three additional titles in this collection.

Chapter 10

Practical Ideas for Eighth Grade

We realize that you will want to focus on your particular grade or subject when you are planning your lessons and implementing CCSS, so we have organized the Practical Ideas chapters by grade level and subject. Each grade starts with an overview followed by ELA technology standards with accompanying apps, software, and websites that you can use to help your students succeed with that standard. We then continue with the math standard for the grade level and review appropriate resources. Finally, we have included some sample lessons for each grade level in various subject areas. Although we have organized the book so you can find your specific grade and subject easily, please do not disregard other sections of this chapter. It is often helpful to see what the standards require before and after the grade you teach. To see grades other than 6-8, look for our three additional titles in this collection, as they could provide information to help you differentiate for students at all levels of your class.

The CCSS has been set up to encourage cross-curricular work in English Language Arts from Grades 6-8. Many of the same standards are used throughout all three grade levels, making it imperative for all three levels of teachers to work closely together to make sure that a spiral effect takes place. Many schools have block planning so that teachers of the same grade level can plan together; however, you may have to get creative to find time when teachers from all three levels can meet. You will need to discuss with your administrators how this will be possible in order to ensure that these technology standards, which are embedded in language arts, reading, and writing, are addressed without overlapping to provide meaningful experiences for your students. Some suggestions are to meet during school or district professional planning days, during the summer (we know many districts that pay for curriculum and unit writing during the summer), during staff meetings, or better yet, to build time into the schedule at the beginning of the year.

Math is also an area where the technological tools become more varied and complex as students advance. The math standards are meant to be embedded in and a natural part of the units your students will be studying. Choosing the correct mathematical tools will be come an important part of your class's learning. There are wonderful new math resources available to help students become proficient in the standards, especially in the area of technology.

We have pulled out the eighth grade standards that include technology for you, and listed them in this chapter so that you have them at your fingertips. Eighth graders are expected to use technology to enhance their literacy skills, such as analyzing the extent to which a filmed or live production of a story or drama stays faithful to or departs from the text or script. They will be required to use digital texts and multimedia to help with reading comprehension, and be able to organize information. Writing is also important, using the internet to find sources of information, and then using publishing sources to publish their work in and out of the classroom. An emphasis on finding needed information quickly and efficiently, and evaluating these sources as well as taking notes, documenting, linking as well as citing sources, and presenting their findings in a multimedia presentation, will be expected. Using tools such as digital dictionaries and thesauruses, as well as read-along texts, is also emphasized. Technology should also be used to practice math skills, and students will need to use digital mathematical tools, which are available through software programs, apps, or websites.

Reading Literature Resources

RL.8.7	READING LITERATURE

Analyze the extent to which a **filmed** or live production of a story or drama stays faithful to or departs from the text or script, evaluating the choices made by the director or actors.

THIS IS A FUN AND CREATIVE STANDARD! Many classic stories have been turned into movies or live productions. Shakespeare is of course the most popular. Most of his plays are still acted out around the world and have become film productions. Jane Austen is another popular classic author who has had most of her books turned into film. Another book turned movie is Little Women, which has had several movie versions. Other classics have their own movies, such as Black Beauty (director Caroline Thompson), Robinson Crusoe (directors Rodney K. Hardy, George Miller), Lord of the Rings (director Peter Jackson), Chronicles of Narnia (director Andrew Adamson), Disney classics such as Where the Red Fern Grows (Director: Lyman Dayton, Sam Pillsbury) and Old Yeller (director Robert Stevenson), The Great Gatsby (director Jack Clayton), Of Mice and Men (director Gary Sinise), Jane Eyre (director Franco Zeffirelli), The Scarlet Letter (director Roland Joffé), and the newest, 12 Years a Slave (director Steve McQueen). The list goes on. You can find many of these books turned into movies simply by using a search engine. Many of these movies can be found at your local library, downloaded from a movie site such as Netflix, or bought them at places such as Amazon. You can find "live" productions that were prerecorded and use those if going to the theater is not an option. The standard asks that these films be compared to the original story or drama and for an evaluation of the choices made by the director or actors. This can of course be done the old-fashioned way by using paper and pencil or a word processor. Or, your students can get creative and make their own video of these comparisons using practically any of your electronic devices, and even do some acting of their favorite parts to be made into a short clip using movie-making software that we recommend below.

Informational Text Resources

RI.8.7	READING INFORMATIONAL TEXT

Evaluate the advantages and disadvantages of using **different mediums** (e.g., print or **digital text, video, multimedia**) to present a particular topic or idea.

THIS STANDARD BEGINS IN KINDERGARTEN with comparing illustrations and text and then grows through the grades using all types of media to compare, support, and analyze the story's meaning. So, the standard is essentially to get meaning from more than the text. Meaning can also come from all the accompanying media and even the format of the story.

Traditionally Microsoft PowerPoint has been the presentation of choice. There is now an individual version called Microsoft Online that includes PowerPoint, but it can be expensive. While this is still a great program to use, other, similar presentation programs have emerged. Apple offers **Keynote (www.apple.com/mac/keynote/)**, which costs $14.99, but the iPad/iPod version is only $4.99. Its features are very similar to PowerPoint. Another program that has emerged is Google Slides. It is aimed toward business presentations; however, the best thing about it is, it is free and web based. It is also very easy to share, and multiple users can work on it at once, even from home, which makes this an especially good program to use when interacting and collaborating with others. You are also able to add audio recordings to your slides as well as visual displays such as pictures and short video clips. Creating student multimedia presentations and presenting them to the class allows the class to analyze how visual and multimedia elements of the presentation contribute to the meaning, tone or beauty of a text. Following are a few presentation tools we recommend.

PRESENTATION SOFTWARE, APPS AND WEBSITES

- **iMovie and iMovie Trailer (www.apple.com/ios/imovie/):** This app ($4.99), which also comes as a program, has many uses in the classroom to create full edited videos or short (90-second) trailers. The trailers can be very useful for focusing on important events and issues, or recounting and presenting ideas to others. The full program is $14.99.

- **MovieMaker (www.moviemaker.com):** This is Microsoft's version of iMovie. It comes standard with any Windows computer.

- **Prezi (www.prezi.com):** You can sign up for a free educational account, and your students can create and share presentations online. Prezi has mind-mapping, zoom, and motion and can import files. Presentations can be downloaded. A Prezi viewer app is available.

- **BaiBoard (www.baiboard.com):** This whiteboard app allows students to create, collaborate, and share, and it's free. The difference between this and other whiteboard apps is that multiple students can have real-time access to one project and collaborate together.

- **Evernote (www.evernote.com):** This is an app, which also allows your students to share notes as well as audio and video recordings. It's very easy to use and share with other students as well as the teacher.

- **PBS Learning Media (pbslearningmedia.org):** This site is a great source for classroom-ready, free digital resources at all grades and in all subjects.

- **Explain Everything (www.explaineverything.com):** This $2.99 app uses text, video, pictures, and voice to present whatever your students are asked to create.

Students can animate, draw, or import almost any file and share multiple ways. It is a top app for a reason. Educational pricing is available.

Reading History Resources

> **RH.6-8.7** | READING HISTORY
>
> Integrate **visual information** (e.g., in charts, graphs, **photographs, videos,** or maps) with other information in print and **digital texts.**

A MULTIMEDIA STORY IS SOME combination of text, still photographs, video clips, audio, graphics, and interactivity presented on a Web site in a nonlinear format in which the information in each medium is complementary, not redundant. They allow the integration of visual information into information in print and digital texts. Following are a few examples of these sites.

MULTIMEDIA WEBSITES

- **CNN (www.cnn.com):** The Cable News Network site is free but includes ads. It has trending news events and access to text, pictures, and video of current events.

- **The Washington Post (www.washingtonpost.com):** This is the official site of the leading newspaper in our capital. There is access to current events in the nation and world. The site is free but does have ads.

- **NPR (www.npr.org):** This site from National Public Radio is government sponsored and so is free with no ads. There are links to current stories with media. Students can listen to the most recent NPR Hourly Newscast.

- **MSNBC (www.msnbc.com):** Another cable news site from NBC Universal, this free site does contain ads. You can find all the day's national and world news including video, text, and print.

Your students can produce multimedia sites as well. Creating their own website is a wonderful way to fulfill this standard. You can find many programs that allow you to create professional looking webpages free. The following are just a few choices.

WEBSITES TO CREATE WEBPAGES

- **Weebly (www.weebly.com):** This is an online website creator that is drag-and-drop easy and includes templates. The basics, which include five pages, are free. There is even an app available.

- **Wix (www.wix.com):** This online website creator is also drag-and-drop easy and includes templates. The basics are free. An app is available.

- **Webs (www.webs.com):** This online website creator allows you to choose a template and then drag and drop elements onto webpages. Basic functionality is free, and an app is available.

- **Kafafa (www.kafafa.com):** This is still another online website creator that is drag-and-drop easy and includes templates. The website is $9.99/month for a class.

- **Shutterfly (http://tinyurl.com/5wjpu7):** Manage parent communication, post important reminders, receive auto reminders for events and volunteer duties, share class photos and videos from daily activities and field trips—all free. It's private and secure. Free apps are also available.

Technical Reading Resources

RST.6-8.9	READING HISTORY

Compare and contrast the information gained from experiments, **simulations, video,** or **multimedia sources** with that gained from reading a text on the same topic.

THERE ARE SO MANY PLACES currently where you can go to get videos showing a variety of educational topics. Anyone and everyone puts up videos— it's up to you to sift through them to find what you are looking for from reliable sources.

EDUCATIONAL VIDEO WEBSITES

- **YouTube (www.youtube.com):** There are many short, free videos that your students can watch, including folktales, science, and people reading popular books that are in your classroom. Your students can listen and then ask and answer questions. There is also a free app.

- **WatchKnowLearn (www.watchknowlearn.org):** The site has many free educational videos that allow you access to everything from frog dissection simulations to earthquake destruction. It organizes content by age ranges and provides reviews.

- **NeoK12 (www.neok12.com):** There are many science experiments, simulations, and videos on all sorts of topics on this website. It also guarantees that all videos are kid safe, and as an added bonus, it is free.

- **EarthCam (www.earthcam.com):** This interesting site allows you to go to many different sites around the world and view video from a live camera (for example, Times Square or Wrigley Field).

- **iTunesU (http://tinyurl.com/lbjbarh):** As stated on their website, "Choose from more than 750,000 free lectures, videos, books, and other resources on thousands of subjects from Algebra to Zoology." It is accessed free through iTunes. A free iTunesU app is also available.

- **BrainPOP (www.brainpop.com):** This website has been around for a long time and is still an oldie but goodie, as it gives educational videos on multiple educational topics, in a fun, cartoon format. Price is $85 to $145.

Using these various sources, it will be easy to have students compare and contrast the information they have gotten from videos and simulations to information they glean from web pages or textbooks. Gathering information has never been so engaging!

Writing Resources

W.8.2a | WRITING

Introduce a topic clearly, previewing what is to follow; organize ideas, concepts, and information into broader categories; include formatting (e.g., headings), graphics (e.g., charts, tables), and **multimedia when useful** to aiding comprehension.

W.8.6 | WRITING

Use technology, including the Internet, to produce and publish writing and present the relationships between information and ideas efficiently as well as to interact and collaborate with others.

WHST.6-8.6 | WRITING HISTORY, SCIENCE AND TECHNICAL SUBJECTS

Use technology, including the Internet, to produce and publish writing and present the relationships between information and ideas clearly and efficiently.

WHST.6-8.8 | WRITING HISTORY, SCIENCE AND TECHNICAL SUBJECTS

Gather relevant information from multiple print and **digital sources,** using search terms effectively; assess the credibility and accuracy of each source; and quote or paraphrase the data and conclusions of others while avoiding plagiarism and following a standard format for citation.

WHST.6-8.2a | WRITING HISTORY, SCIENCE AND TECHNICAL SUBJECTS

Introduce a topic clearly, previewing what is to follow; organize ideas, concepts, and information into broader categories as appropriate to achieving purpose; including formatting (e.g., headings), graphics (e.g., charts, tables), and **multimedia when useful** to aiding comprehension.

BY THE TIME STUDENTS ARE IN EIGHTH GRADE, they should be able to search the internet independently to gather the information that they need on a given topic. Your class may need some reminders on effective searching, so lessons on internet searching are critical, as well as lessons on media literacy. Media literacy is especially crucial, as students now need to be able to critique a website before using it—anyone can put up a webpage. They will also need to be able to assess the credibility and accuracy of each source, and quote or paraphrase the data and conclusions of others while avoiding plagiarism. We discuss these techniques in the following paragraphs.

Although students are sufficiently net-savvy these days, and have done a lot of searching in previous grades, eighth graders still need assistance with the basics of searching. Various search engines work differently, and each will return different information. Therefore, your students need to know how to use multiple engines.

Smart searching will help avoid a lot of wasted time. Teaching students to analyze search results will definitely help them find better information and think more critically about any information they find on the internet. Following are a few suggestions to share with your students.

- Choose your search terms carefully. Be precise about what you are looking for, though you should use phrases and not full sentences.

- Adding more words can narrow a search. Use Boolean searches to narrow your topic with quotation marks. There's a big difference between "gopher" and "habitats of gophers in North America."

- Use synonyms! If kids can't find what they're looking for, have them try keywords that mean the same thing or are related.

- Type "site." Typing "site:" (with the colon) after your keyword and before a URL will tell many search engines to search within a specific website.

- Add a minus sign. Adding a minus sign (a hyphen) immediately before any word, with no space in between, indicates that you don't want that word to appear in your search results. For example, "Saturn -cars" will give you information about the planet, not the automobile.

Using tried and true methods for taking notes and paraphrasing and summarizing information from books can still be used to gather information and take notes on websites. Teaching students to use data sheets, note cards, and KWL (Know, What, Learn) techniques still works; however, there are now ways that technology can help and sometimes make it easier. The **Kentucky Virtual Library** is a good website to use as a resource for some of these techniques. Evernote is a wonderful app that allows students to take notes and to import a worksheet, document, or picture, including a snapshot of a webpage, then annotate it using tools that you would use with interactive whiteboard software. It lets them highlight words, cut and paste, and add sticky notes. The sticky notes are especially useful to summarize or paraphrase students' notes. It also allows them to use voice recognition. They can then send their annotated sheet to someone else (including the teacher). Another way to take notes is using the "add-on" for your internet browser. The free add-on Diigo (www.diigo.com) is made for note taking on docs, pdfs, and screenshots, and for saving found sites and documents as resources to take notes on later with annotations and highlighting.

Modeling is, of course, essential when you are teaching your students how to glean information from a website. Your interactive whiteboard is a perfect tool for modeling your lesson. Don't have an interactive whiteboard? Use **RealtimeBoard** **(www.realtimeboard.com)**. It's a free website that allows you to turn an ordinary whiteboard into an interactive one. All you need is a computer and a projector! Using the many tools an interactive whiteboard and software have to offer will really help teach your students how to navigate through information posted on the internet.

Using mind-mapping tools when gathering information will help your students organize their research.

APPS AND WEBSITES FOR MIND-MAPPING

- **Inspiration (http://tinyurl.com/ygharef):** A mind-mapping software program that helps student organize their writing. It can be especially helpful for students who are learning to create paragraphs and organize big ideas into their smaller parts. $40 to $640. Their web-based version is called **Webspiration (http://tinyurl.com/bmop3nh)**. $6/month.

- **Popplet (www.popplet.com):** A wonderful online organizational tool for students' writing. A free app called **Popplet Lite** is also available. It is easy to use, and students can import pictures and text to create web maps.

- **Bubbl.us (www.bubbl.us):** This is a free (with limited use) mind-mapping website for Grades K–12. It can be shared by multiple students at a time and comes with an app. For more options, purchase a package for $6/month or $59/year. Both come with a 30-day free trial. Site licensing is available. Contact the company for specifics.

- **Mindmeister (www.mindmeister.com/education):** This is a free, basic mind-mapping website for Grades 2–12. Upgrades are available ($18/month for a single user; $30 per user for 6 months). Educational pricing is available for schools and universities ($6 per user for 6 months). All of the upgrades have a free trial period.

- **FreeMind (http://tinyurl.com/5qrd5):** This is a free mind-mapping tool for Grades 2–12. FreeMind is written in Java and will run on almost any system with a Java runtime environment. Options for a basic or maximum install are available.

Of course, word documents such as what comes with Microsoft Office, Apple, or Google Docs (to name a few) can also be used. Some teachers also make digital templates to help students find specific information and to help students organize their notes, with spaces to summarize or paraphrase.

Eighth graders will also need to provide basic bibliographic information for sources. Of course, making your own template and having the students fill it in using a word processing program works; however, there are some websites that can be used, such as EasyBib, Citation Machine, or StyleWizard.

Producing and publishing writing digitally is another standard eighth graders are expected to meet. There are many websites out there that allow you to publish student writing. Using blogging websites such as **Edmodo (www.edmodo.com), TeacherBlogIt (www.teacherblogit.com)**, and **Wikispaces (www.wikispaces.com)** are other ways to share students' writing in a safe, protected environment and an excellent way to interact and collaborate with others. These sites allow teachers to set themselves up as administrators and add students to various groups. All of the students' writing is kept secure in these groups.

You can give assignments asking for short answers where everyone can respond, or you can ask them to write longer assignments on their own. They can then work on assignments and submit privately to you, or post them on the site to share.

Following are sites that ask students to submit their work for publication.

PUBLISHING WEBSITES

- **Scholastic Publishing: (http://tinyurl.com/plwnn6f):** A free website where teachers can submit student writing for publication.

- **PBS Kids Writing (pbskids.org/writerscontest/):** This free site asks for student writing and serves as a nice incentive to get students to do their best writing.

- **Lulu (www.lulu.com) and Lulu Jr (www.lulujr.com):** These sites allow you to create real books and publish them online. Parents can purchase the books as a keepsake. The site is free to use, but a fee is required to publish .

- **TikaTok (www.tikatok.com):** This is another site that allows students to write, create, and publish stories as ebooks or hardcover books. TikaTok Story Spark is an app that you can purchase for $3. Classroom price for TikaTok starts at $19 a year.

- **Cast UDL Book Builder (http://bookbuilder.cast.org/):** This is a free site that lets you publish your ebook and see what others have published.

- **Poetry Idea Engine from Scholastic (http://tinyurl.com/nm2gtba):** The site allows you to use templates to make different forms of poetry, another great way technology gets kids writing. Better still, it is free!

Following are some apps that allow students to create shorter versions of their stories in an animated way.

APPS AND WEBSITES USING ANIMATION

- **iFunFace (www.ifunface.com):** Students can create a read-aloud to show how the main idea and details flow by using a photo and audio recording to create an animation. This helps students visualize how to support details that branch off from the main ideas and how they all flow together. The app is free but can be upgraded for $1.99.

- **Blabberize (www.blabberize.com):** Students can speak the text and use photos to illustrate it in an animated format. Free.

- **Voki (www.voki.com):** Students can use their voices to speak the text, and photos can be used to illustrate in an animated format. It is free, but there are ads.

- **Fotobabble (www.fotobabble.com):** Students' voices can speak the text, and photos can be used to illustrate. Free.

These are not conducive to stories in paragraph form; however, you can use your voice to speak the text, and photos can be used to illustrate in an animated format.

Speaking and Listening Resources

SL.8.2	SPEAKING AND LISTENING

Analyze the purpose of information presented in **diverse media and formats** (e.g., visually, quantitatively, orally) and evaluate the motives (e.g., social, commercial, political) behind its presentation

SL.8.5	SPEAKING AND LISTENING

Integrate **multimedia and visual displays** into presentations to clarify information, strengthen claims and evidence, and add interest.

MICROSOFT POWERPOINT IS OFTEN the presentation software of choice. There is now an individual version called Microsoft Online that includes Power-Point. Although this is still a great program to use, other presentation programs have emerged. Apple offers **Keynote (www.apple.com/mac/keynote/)** as part of their software package with computers, but the iPad/iPod version does cost. Another program that has emerged is the **Google Slides (www.google.com/slides/about/)**. There are other resources that help with presentations, such as **Microsoft Draw (www.office.com)** and **Google Drawings (www.google.com/drive)**. Office is aimed toward business presentations; however, Google Drive products such as Slides and Drawings are free and web based. Slides is also very easy to share, and multiple users can work on a document at once, which makes this an especially good program to use when interacting and collaborating with others. Students can also add audio recordings to their slides, as well as visual displays such as pictures and short video clips. You could also have your students use the following digital tools to develop their speaking and listening skills.

APPS, SOFTWARE, AND WEBSITES TO CREATE SLIDESHOWS AND MOVIES

- **iMovie (www.apple.com/ios/imovie/):** This app ($4.99), which also comes as a program, has many uses in the classroom to create full edited videos or short 1-minute trailers. The trailers can be very useful for recounting and presenting ideas to others.

- **Animoto (www.animoto.com):** This website allows you to turn your photos and music into stunning video slideshows. Educational use is free for unlimited videos of 20 minutes.

- **MovieMaker (www.moviemaker.com):** This is Microsoft's version of iMovie. It comes standard with any Windows computer.

- **Prezi (www.prezi.com):** You can sign up for a free educational account, and your students can create and share presentations online. Prezi has mind-mapping, zoom, and motion, and it can import files. Presentations can be downloaded. A Prezi viewer app is available.

- **Wideo (www.wideo.co [.co not .com]):** Wideo allows you to easily make animation videos. Education pricing is $0.75/month.

- **Explain Everything (www.explaineverything.com):** This $2.99 app uses text, video, pictures, and voice to present whatever your students are asked to create. They can illustrate a story or poem or recount information they hear.

- **Stupeflix (https://studio.stupeflix.com/en/):** Make free movies using your photos and videos for up to 20 minutes. It's easy, and a lot of fun!

- **SchoolTube (www.schooltube.com):** This is educators' best free source for a video-sharing community where students can watch or post videos.

- **WebQuests (www.webquest.org)** are great tools to use for presentations. Web-Quest is a website that allows students to follow an already-created, project-based lesson where information is found solely on the internet. You can also create your own WebQuest if you have a website-building program or a website like **Kafafa (www.kafafa.com/kafafa)**. WebQuest.org is the original and most popular site; however, if you search the internet, you will find more sites that you can use.

Language Resources

L.8.4c	LANGUAGE
Consult general and specialized reference materials (e.g., dictionaries, glossaries, thesauruses), both print and **digital**, to find the pronunciation of a word or determine or clarify its precise meaning or its part of speech.	

ALTHOUGH DIGITAL DICTIONARIES and thesauruses are not updated as often as digital encyclopedias, they are still very convenient to use and are kept current. These sites should be bookmarked or put on your website for easy access. The more students use them, the more comfortable they will become. You should do lessons and activities to learn and practice the necessary skills with an online dictionary.

DIGITAL DICTIONARY AND THESAURUS WEBSITES

- **Merriam-Webster (www.merriam-webster.com):** A free digital dictionary for all ages. It is the most commonly used digital dictionary and includes a thesaurus.

- **WordSmyth (www.wordsmyth.net):** This site shows three levels of a student dictionary. When looking up a word, you also see also links to a thesaurus and rhyming dictionary for that word. You can sign up for an ad-free version, which will not cost your school.

- **Word Central Kids (www.wordcentral.com):** A student online dictionary that includes an audio pronunciation of the word as well as the definition. There are many teacher resources.

- **Thesaurus.com (www.thesaurus.com):** This is a fine thesaurus site with many extra features. It does have some ads, but it is available online and as an app. The site is free.

Using the app or website **Trading Cards (http://tinyurl.com/8lqftek)** is a good way to document vocabulary words by adding their definitions and a picture, and recording voices for pronunciation. You can also use Trading Cards by doing an activity with an online thesaurus. You can give a student a word on a trading card, and then ask them to make as many trading cards as they can of synonyms and antonyms of that word. Students can print these out and trade them with others, or make them into a digital book. The app Explain Everything is also easy to use to import a picture, record your voice, and make a digital presentation.

Math Resources

MP5	MATH
Use appropriate **tools** strategically.	

THERE ARE TWO MAIN SETS of standards, processes and practices, for the Common Core Math standards. First, you have the math targets, written similarly to ELA (The Number System, Expressions & Equations, Functions, Geometry, and Statistics & Probability). While you work with eighth grade students on mathematical processes, such as Expressions & Equations or Geometry, you need to teach your students how to apply the Standards for Mathematical Practices (which include problem solving and precision) to those processes. One practice, the only one that includes technology, is mathematical practice 5, "Use appropriate tools strategically."

Following is the explanation CCSS provides for **MP5**. As this is the standard explanation for Grades K–12, it does include references to higher grades.

> Mathematically proficient students consider the available tools when solving a mathematical problem. These tools might include pencil and paper, concrete models, a ruler, a protractor, **a calculator, a spreadsheet, a computer algebra system, a statistical package, or dynamic geometry software**. Proficient students are sufficiently familiar with tools appropriate for their grade or course to make sound decisions about when each of these tools might be helpful, recognizing both the insight to be gained and their limitations. For example, mathematically proficient high school students analyze graphs of functions and solutions generated using a **graphing calculator**. They detect possible errors by strategically using estimation and other mathematical knowledge. When making mathematical models, they know that **technology** can enable them to visualize the results of

varying assumptions, explore consequences, and compare predictions with data. Mathematically proficient students at various grade levels are able to identify relevant external mathematical resources, such as **digital content located on a website**, and use them to pose or solve problems. They are able to use technological tools to explore and deepen their understanding of concepts.

Because this description did not give examples for all grades, we have listed appropriate apps, websites, software, and lessons that will help translate this standard for eighth grade.

Currently, this is the only eighth grade math standard that involves technology. Since using any kind of technology to have students practice math can grab their attention, help long-term learning, and make math fun, technology is a math tool students should use as much as possible. There are many math programs, websites, and apps out there, which allow students to explore and deepen their understanding of math concepts. The best of them have students learning in creative ways and are not just electronic worksheets. They automatically adapt to the students skill level, and they give you the data you need to know where students are in their learning and what they need to effectively continue. Following are many good math resources. Some are free. Some are not. Unfortunately, the free resources, many with ads, are usually less interesting to your students and are not as well organized. They don't give you the feedback you need. It is up to you to decide what is best for your circumstances and budget.

Following are some resources we recommend that you can use to enhance the eighth grade math standards.

HOW-TO APPS AND WEBSITES

- **VirtualNerd (www.virtualnerd.com):** This is a free website with well-made videos on math subjects through Algebra 2 that you can use for instruction or to flip the classroom.

- **Khan Academy (www. khanacademy.org):** This is a free website provided by a nonprofit organization. It has excellent activities at all age levels, including high school. Once logged in, you can keep track of student progress and data easily.

- **IXL (www.ixl.com/math/):** This online site features adaptive individualized math through gameplay. It gives students immediate feedback and covers many skills, despite its emphasis on drills. Levels go to Algebra 2. Class price is $199/year.

- **Programs such as Microsoft Excel (www.office.com), Apple Numbers (www.**

apple.com/mac/numbers/), or **Google Sheets (www.google.com/sheets/about/)** are good ways to teach students about charts and graphs. Making charts and graphs is a great way to learn how to interpret and present information.

- **Gliffy (www.gliffy.com):** Create professional-quality flowcharts, wireframes, diagrams, and more. Free for limited use. Upgrades available for a fee.

- **Create-a-Graph (http://tinyurl.com/yoedjn):** Create bar, line, area, pie, and XY graphs with this free website. It is easy to use, and you can print, save or email your completed graphs.

- **ClassTools (www.classtools.net):** Create graphs and charts (and use many other helpful classroom tools like a QR code generator or timeline!) with this free website.

- **Edhead (www.edheads.org):** Real-world medical and engineering scenarios will intrigue kids on this free website. The site adeptly weaves content into authentic simulations. In-activity definitions and glossaries provide solid vocabulary support. There is no ability to monitor progress, and students can't fast forward/rewind within segments.

- **Algebra Touch (www.regularberry.com):** This intuitive app makes learning algebra easy. Teachers can track students' progress, and it is especially great for struggling students. The price is $2.99.

- **MathPickle (www.mathpickle.com):** This free website for Grades 5–12 is loaded with math challenges, puzzling games, videos for flipping the classroom, and great ideas. There is a lot here, and you might need to guide your students through, unless they are very independent.

- **GeoGebra (www.geogebra.org):** Although it will take some time for teachers and students to learn how to use the site, if they are willing to put in the time, GeoGebra offers endless math learning possibilities. The site is free and for Grades 7–12.

- **iCrosss (http://tinyurl.com/phsouuf):** This $0.99 app will help students learn solid geometry in an easy and funny way. Spin and rotate shapes, and create cross sections to boost spatial understanding of geometric solids.

- **Algodoo (www.algodoo.com):** This free app is a virtual sandbox tool that helps your students play with the concepts of physics to design, construct, and explore.

- **Desmos (www.desmos.com/calculator):** This website is a next-generation graphing calculator where students can use a "slider" to change the function and see how that affects the graph. It is an elegant math tool that makes concepts more concrete.

- **Autodesk Digital STEAM Measurement (http://tinyurl.com/na3sn9h):** This app is free and shows students differing ways to measure quantity, dimension, time, temperature, capacity, weight, and mass in real-world situations. It is mostly interactive and teaches international measurement.

- **Get the Math (http://tinyurl.com/ne8fo6n):** This is a free website through PBS that uses video games, music, fashion, sports, restaurants, and special effects to teach math concepts. It is targeted for teenagers and has some great challenges, videos, and resources. It includes resources for teachers.

- **Study Island (www.studyisland.com):** This is a web-based program where students work on engaging, interactive lessons and activities at their own pace to learn aligned Common Core math standards. Teachers can also choose to guide students and assign specific areas to work through. This program must be purchased. Pricing information is available on the website.

- **DreamBox Learning Math (www.dreambox.com):** Individualized, adaptive, game-based math that keeps kids coming back for more. Available online or through an app. Price is $12.95/month (home) or $25/month (school), less if packaged.

- **Radix Endeavor (www.radixendeavor.org):** This is multiplayer online game play for STEM learning. Students are the players and play in the math or science strand. Teachers can enroll classes, but enrollment is not necessary for students to play this free role-playing math game created by MIT.

- **TenMarks (www.tenmarks.com):** This website is adaptable to each student's math skill level. It is free for a single class, but schools and districts pay $20 per student for premium features. Has instruction, practice, and even assessment modeled after PARCC.

- **HippoCampus (www.gippocampus.org):** The ways to use this free website vary greatly. It has high school and college level math, but also English, social studies, science, and even religion. There are also assessments, teacher resources such as rubrics, tips about teaching, and so on. You must dig to find some of the great resources, but they are well worth it.

- **Gooru (Gooru.org):** This is a free website with a supportive app available for free. The idea of the site is to share information and to make great resources available globally. The site covers math, science, social studies, and language arts by providing videos, worksheet, assessments, and other resources for students, broken out by standard. Great for flipping the classroom. This is for Grades K–12.

- **Math Open Reference (www.mathopenref.com):** This is a free website with a myriad resources for teachers to use with their students. The site does have ads.

Literacy Lessons

Cross-curriculum planning is encouraged with the Common Core by using ELA standards in history, science, and technical subjects. However, we encourage you to go further and include the arts, math, and physical education teachers in your planning. How will you ever get through everything if you teach standard by standard? The key to planning with the CCSS is to teach multiple standards in one lesson, when you can. We hope that the following list of a few sample lessons for eighth grade will inspire you to become an effective technology lesson planner.

VOCABULARY

From the files of our eighth grade friends, this vocabulary lesson is done in conjunction with reading a novel or nonfiction text. As you know, vocabulary plays a vital role in reading comprehension. This lesson is a fun way to aid vocabulary development. Before you begin the book, develop a list of key vocabulary words for the first few chapters. Students consult digital and print reference materials to understand and learn what words mean, as well as use them in sentences. (See our list of suggested materials under **L.8.4c.**) This satisfies **L.8.4c.** Next, students pick a way to present their vocabulary words, definitions, and sentences (Prezi, Trading Cards, iMovie Trailer, Explain Everything, etc.). Teams present and project (RealtimeBoard) to the class, making sure they save time for asking and answering any questions, as they are "the experts" on the vocabulary words. These presentations can then be uploaded to YouTube or any other way you may have to share with absent students and/or parents! They can then be used to review later, or could be great for flipping the classroom. Our former eighth grade colleagues repeated this process for the remainder of the book. Students were encouraged to try a different technology method each time. Some students may even ask to try new technology! **RH.6-8.7** is satisfied, as students should be encouraged to include visual information in their presentations (graphics and even music). Students are introducing, producing, and publishing writing, as well as working together to present their ideas clearly and efficiently, so **WHST.6-8.2a**, **W.8.2a**, **W.8.6**, and **WHST.6-8.6** are also met. **RI.8.7** and **W.8.8** are satisfied when students gather, integrate, and present their information, in an original way. Using diverse media and formats (including music, graphics, voice-overs, etc.) to present and clarify information is definitely a part of this project, so **SL.8.2** and **SL.8.5** are also fulfilled.

SHAKESPEARE

This next intriguing lesson has students studying Shakespeare by reading a work by Shakespeare and then watching a film or live production of the same play. Really, however, this lesson can be done with any film or live production to support a text. (See our text/video suggestions under **RL.8.7**.) Next, students take notes (using Evernote or the Kentucky Virtual Library) on where the video or live production stayed faithful to or departed from the text. Encourage students to look up any words, terms, or phrases they are unfamiliar with. Using any word processing software of their choosing, students write an analysis of these differences and similarities, offering a personal reflection on choices made by the actors and/or directors. In addition, students need to evaluate the advantages and disadvantages of a medium different from the text to present their text's theme, thus satisfying standard **RI.8.7** and **L.8.4c**. Conversely, this document now serves as their "blueprint" for the technology phase of this lesson. Next, students create a wiki (complete with visual information) comparing and contrasting their text to the film or live production. Ideas on the wiki or blog should be well organized, including headings, appropriate graphics, and charts, tables (if needed), and perhaps even short snippets of the film or live production to illustrate their point. This lesson has also satisfied **RH.6-8.7**, **RST.6-8.9**, **W.8.2a**, **W.8.6**, **WHST.6-8.2a**, and **WHST.6-8.6**. Encourage students to gather any information, from multiple print and digital sources, that will help to support their analysis and stance, making sure they cite references accurately and correctly (**WHST.6-8.8** is thus satisfied). Before wikis are uploaded to YouTube (or any sharing method you prefer), students should present their findings to the class. RealtimeBoard would be great for this! When each presentation is complete, presenters should field questions and/or constructive comments from the audience, defending and strengthening their position, or clarifying anything that needs further explanation. Doing so will satisfy both speech standards (**SL.8.2** and **SL.8.5**). This significant lesson satisfies many standards and helps students further their technology knowledge by creating and maintaining wikis.

Social Studies/Science Lessons

The following sample lessons address CCSS ELA standards and teach lessons based on national standards in social studies and science.

GREAT DEPRESSION

A local eighth grade class in our former district had great fun with this social studies WebQuest on the Great Depression, which they adapted from a WebQuest developed by a Kansas middle school. Do a Google search for Great Depression WebQuests, or make your own using Google Sites or your favorite website design software, app, or online provider. Students work in teams to come up with a plan to prevent the Great Depression. An intriguing idea is to make teams of four, with each member having a different role—the economist, the historian, the policy analyst, or the biographer. Each team member needs to make sure they fulfill their role—not only will they have to share their information with other members, but the entire team will present their preventative solutions to the class. In class, have a discussion about the Great Depression, its causes, and so forth. Bring in as many different sources (texts, videos, movies, etc.) to facilitate this discussion. You will also need many websites covering a multitude of Great Depression aspects. Teams travel back in time to 1928 and research what life was like at that time, leading up to the Great Depression. During their research, teams take notes (Evernote or the Kentucky Virtual Library) of any and all factors causing the Great Depression. Once students feel their research is complete and they have learned all they can about the causes of the Great Depression, teams develop a plan to keep it from happening. We have outlined specific duties for each role below. See **our website (http://tinyurl.com/ oexfhcv)** for a list of resources for this lesson.

The Economist. One facet of the Great Depression was the sudden drop in the stock market (the Great Crash). Your mission is to find out what events triggered the crash. Prepare a presentation (PowerPoint, Keynote, iMovie Trailer, Prezi, etc.) outlining what you think triggered the Great Crash, as well as your thoughts on how it could have been prevented. You may want to give the economists some guiding questions.

For their research, economists will need a variety of sources—text, websites, videos, and so on. Students also need to be encouraged to look up in reference materials any words or terms they are unfamiliar with, as well as cite appropriately all of the sources they used (thus satisfying standard **L.8.4c**). These are only a few suggestions for economists to use for their research. You will want to provide more to guide them in their work.

The Historian. As the historian, students will explain the extent and depth of business failures, unemployment, and poverty during the Depression. Prepare a presentation (PowerPoint, Keynote, iMovie Trailer, Prezi, etc.) outlining a history of events leading to the stock market crash and Great Depression, as well as your thoughts on how it could have been prevented. You may want to give the historians some guiding questions.

To help historians with their research, they will need a variety of sources, text, websites, videos, and so on. Students also need to be encouraged to look up in reference materials any words or terms they are unfamiliar with, as well as cite appropriately all of the sources they used (thus satisfying standard **L.8.4c**). These are only a few suggestions for historians to use for their research. You will want to provide more to guide them in their work.

The Policy Analyst. The mission of the policy analyst is to learn about the New Deal and how it impacted the Depression and the role of the government in the economy. Prepare a presentation (PowerPoint, Keynote, iMovie Trailer, Prezi, etc.) outlining a history of events leading to the stock market crash, the Great Depression, and the New Deal, as well as your thoughts on how it could have been prevented. Policy analysts may want to work closely with the economist and historian. You may want to give the policy analysts some guiding questions.

To help policy analysts with their research, they will need a variety of sources, text, websites, videos, and so on. Students also need to be encouraged to look up in reference materials any words or terms they are unfamiliar with, as well as cite appropriately all of the sources they used (thus satisfying standard **L.8.4c**). These are only a few suggestions for policy analysts to use for their research. You will want to provide more to guide them in their work.

The Biographer. The mission of the biographer is to find out how the following people influenced the time period before, during, and after the Great Depression.

- Will Rogers

- Eleanor Roosevelt

- Franklin Roosevelt

- Charles Lindberg

Prepare a presentation (PowerPoint, Keynote, iMovie Trailer, Prezi, etc.) detailing each of the people listed and what role they played, as well as your thoughts on what each of them could have done to prevent the Great Depression. You may want to give the biographers some guiding questions.

To help biographers with their research, they will need a variety of sources, text, websites, videos, and so on. Students also need to be encouraged to look up in reference materials any words or terms they are unfamiliar with, as well as cite appropriately all of the sources they used (thus satisfying standard **L.8.4c**). These are only a few suggestions for historians to use for their research. You will want to provide more to guide them in their work.

Students should present their findings to the class. Using RealtimeBoard would be great for this! After each presentation is complete, presenters should field questions and/or constructive comments from the audience, defending, strengthening their position, or clarifying anything that needs further explanation. Doing so would satisfy both speech standards (**SL.8.2** and **SL.8.5**). Other standards this in-depth lesson covers include **RH.6-8.7**, **W.8.2a**, **W.8.6**, **WHST.6-8.6**, **WHST.6-8.8**, and **WHST.6-8.2a.** as students are researching, writing, and organizing ideas, concepts, and information to produce a presentation on their thoughts of how the Great Depression could have been prevented. Students should be encouraged to use headings, charts, and tables (when and where necessary), as well as pictures, graphics, and/or music to enhance their presentations. They may even wish to include short videos.

ENGINEERING

Eighth graders across the country are studying engineering, technology, and applications of science. This lesson is from the file of a middle school teacher and serves as an introduction to one of the science units. In this lesson, students explore the world of engineering (for some this will be an introduction to engineering) and what it means to have a career as an engineer. Start your lesson with a class discussion, learning about your students and their thoughts about what career they may pursue. Lead the conversation toward the career of engineering. You may wish to spark the conversation by asking questions like "Have you ever heard of a career called engineering?"; "What does an engineer do?"; "What do you know about engineering?" or "Do you know someone who is an engineer?" That conversation should then lead into a discussion of different types of engineers. Using your whiteboard to make a list, have students brainstorm different kinds of engineers (mechanical, electrical, chemical, civil, etc.) You may need to bring in some outside sources to help spark this brainstorm session. Encourage students to use print and digital reference materials like Merriam-Webster, Word Central, WordSmyth, or Thesaurus.com. See our detailed explanation under **L.8.4c**, which is also the standard students will be satisfying. Adding a sketch or drawing of the vocabulary term or phrase is a great way for students to internalize the words. Next, you may want to preview engineering by showing students videos. There are many places to search. Please refer to our detailed explanation earlier, under **RST.6-8.9**, (for example: YouTube, WatchKnowLearn, iTunesU, and BrainPOP). Students can use Evernote,

The Kentucky Virtual Library, or Diigo for note taking. See our explanation above at standard **WHST.6-8.2a**, as you can even "share" worksheets and other items with your students. Students can also "share" their work with you. Explain Everything is another good site to use for note taking, as students can write notes or vocabulary definitions and even draw or sketch pictures to go with their words. Once students are comfortable with the vocabulary, explain that the assignment will be to design a presentation about one of the engineering careers you just brainstormed. Before they actually begin their presentation, students need to come up with a list of questions (about their specific engineering category) they wish to find out while researching. Encourage students to dig deeper than "How much money do they make?" This may mean students will need to use resources before doing research, in order to come up with quality questions. There are some excellent websites and videos to consider for students. See **our website (http://tinyurl.com/oexfhcv)** for more ideas.

Next, students design a presentation on their engineering career (PowerPoint, Keynote, iMovie Trailer, Prezi, etc.). Students will be presenting their projects (Real-timeBoard would be great for this), using diverse media and formats (including music, graphics, voice-overs, etc.). After each presentation is complete, presenters should field questions and/or constructive comments from the audience, defending, strengthening their position, or clarifying anything that needs further explanation (thus fulfilling **SL.8.2** and **SL.8.5**). Students listening to the presentations may want to take notes, either for themselves or to share positive feedback with the presenter.

Other standards this in depth lesson covers include **RH.6-8.7**, **W.8.2a**, **W.8.6**, **WHST.6-8.6**, **WHST.6-8.8**, **W.6.2a**, and **WHST.6-8.2a**, as students are researching, writing, and organizing ideas, concepts, and information to produce a presentation about their ideas on the career of engineering. Students should be encouraged to use headings, charts, and tables (when and where necessary), as well as pictures, graphics, and/or music to enhance their presentations. They may even wish to include short videos.

Math Lessons

MATHEMATICS REVIEW

This math lesson, again from the files of one of our middle school friends, is similar to a lesson in seventh grade math. Teachers used this lesson as a review at the end of a semester, but you could use it to review at the end of any unit. Or you can use it as a preview before a lesson ("flipping the classroom.") Teams of students are "experts" on a math topic or skill and will make instructional videos similar to those found at Virtual Nerd or Khan Academy. You may wish to give a pretest in advance of starting a new unit, to determine your "experts" in each area. Or, on the whiteboard, you and your students make a list of all the concepts and skills studied throughout the semester. In pairs or groups of three (depending how many total), students pick a topic they want to "be an expert" on. Using iMovie, MovieMaker, or any other movie-making software, teams begin making their teaching videos. Teams should view several examples from Virtual Nerd or Khan Academy before beginning. Students may also need access to tablets and the whiteboard as they begin to film their lesson. At the appropriate time, have students project their movie and "teach" the class. "Learning" students take notes to use for studying using Evernote, Diigo, Explain Everything (which can be written and voice recorded), and so on. Teams present (RealtimeBoard) to the class, making sure they save time for asking and answering any questions, as they are "the experts" on the math topic. These movies can then be uploaded to YouTube or your favorite posting site to share with absent students and/or parents. They can then be used to review later, or could be great for flipping the classroom. In addition to **MP5**, standard **RH.6-8.7** is satisfied, as students should be encouraged to include visual information in their presentations (graphics and even music). Students are introducing, producing, and publishing writing, as well as working together to present their ideas clearly and efficiently, so **WHST.6-8.2a**, **W.8.2a**, **W.8.6**, and **WHST.6-8.6** are also met. **RI.8.7** and **W.8.8** are also satisfied when students gather, integrate, and present their information, in an original way. Using diverse media and formats (including music, graphics, voice-overs, etc.) to present and clarify information is definitely a part of this project, so **SL.8.2** and **SL.8.5** are also fulfilled.

QUADRATIC EQUATION

This next math lesson comes from the files of our former eighth grade colleagues at the local middle school. Students are introduced to simple quadratic equations, graphing and exploring parabolas. Since this is their first exposure to quadratic equations, you may need to do some vocabulary work and activating schema with the students, before actually beginning your lessons. Providing students with a list of vocabulary words they will encounter when learning about quadratic equations might be helpful. Students can use Evernote, The Kentucky Virtual Library, or Diigo for note taking. See our explanation above under **WHST.6-8.2a**, as you can even "share" worksheets and so on with your students. Students can also "share" their vocabulary work with you. Encourage students to use print and digital reference materials like Merriam-Webster, Word Central, WordSmyth, or Thesaurus.com. See our detailed explanation under **L.8.4c**, which is also the standard students will be satisfying. Adding a sketch or drawing of the vocabulary term or phrase is a great way for students to internalize the words and can easily be done on their tablets, using one of the note taking sites previously mentioned. Next, you may want to preview quadratic equations by showing students videos. There are many places to search for videos on the subject. Please refer to our detailed explanation earlier, under **RST.6-8.9** (for example: YouTube, WatchKnowLearn, iTunesU, BrainPOP, and Khan Academy). As you begin instruction, you may want students to explore or to refresh their minds concerning lines of symmetry, as well as reflecting lines. You can also do this on tablets or computers as well. Microsoft Office's Excel, Apple's Numbers, or Google Sheets is a great way to teach charts and graphs. Making your own charts and graphs is also a good way to learn how to interpret and present information. Gliffy, Create-a-Graph, and ClassTools are free sites you can use. You may also have your own sites to use for graphing. Students will need these graphing sites more as you get deeper into the lesson. By the way, you are satisfying **W.6.2a** when using and applying online graph sites. Next, continue the lesson, having students team up. One student is in charge of using the graphing calculator, while the other sketches and writes. You may want to assign quadratic equations from a textbook, make up an activity sheet, or search online for an activity sheet on quadratic equations already made. Students perform all work on their tablets (which will be submitted to you), making sure they both verify their answer and check to make sure their explanation is clear and complete. Halfway through the assignment, students can switch roles. Also encourage students, if need be, to consult other teams for ideas and suggestions (before asking you, the teacher) as this will satisfy standard **W.8.6** (interacting and working collaboratively with others). Before class ends, bring students back together as a whole group. Put a problem on the board and ask students to answer your questions about the problem. This is the student's "exit slip," as well as your way to check for understanding. Repeat several times so everyone has a chance to show their understanding. You may also try this using Explain Everything, or another of the apps we mentioned previously, and have all students submit all answers to you electronically. Finally, for homework, have students finish the assignment given in class, or hand out another assignment to be done and handed in electronically the next day. In addition to the standards mentioned earlier that will be satisfied with this lesson, if you have students present their quadratic equation work to the class (maybe going over homework and sharing in class the second day) **SL.8.2** and **SL.8.5** will be satisfied. In addition to **MP5**, **W. 8.2a**, **WHST.6-8.6**, and **WHST.6-8.2a** are also satisfied, as students need to write and use their math vocabulary terms learned, correctly and efficiently, as well as write and present their ideas and explanations clearly and succinctly. Finally, **RH.6-8.7** is also satisfied, as teams are using visual information (graphs) to illustrate their written explanations.

A Final Note

As students progress through the grades, they are establishing their baseline of proficiency in technology. This will definitely enhance students' experiences with technology in high school, as well as satisfy the CCSS performance standards at the 6–8 level. We hope that you found the resources and lesson ideas presented in this chapter useful and that they are easy to adapt to your class.

You will find more resources online at **our website (http://tinyurl.com/oexfhcv)**, which may be helpful to you as you look to differentiate your instruction. Visit our website for updated information about this book. To learn more about meeting technology standards found within the CCSS for other grades, look for our three additional titles in this collection.

References

DeWitt, P. (2013, July 7). *Take a risk . . . Flip your parent communication!* [Blog post]. Retrieved from http://blogs.edweek.org/edweek/finding_common_ground/2013/07/take_a_risk_flip_your_parent_communication.html

Edutopia. (2007). What is successful technology integration? *Technology Integration Professional Development Guide.* Retrieved from http://www.edutopia.org/technology-integration-guide-description

Henderson. A., & Mapp, K. (2002). *A new wave of evidence: The impact of school, family, and community connections on student achievement* (Annual Synthesis 2002). Retrieved from Southwest Educational Development Laboratory website: http://www.sedl.org/connections/resources/evidence.pdf

LEAD Commission. (2012). *Parents' and teachers' attitudes and opinions on technology in education.* (National online survey, August 2012). Retrieved from LEAD Commission website: http://www.leadcommission.org/sites/default/files/LEAD Poll Deck.pdf

Meeuwse, K. (2013, April 11). *Using iPads to transform teaching and learning* [Blog post]. Retrieved from http://iteachwithipads.net/2013/04/11/using-ipads-to-transform-teaching-and-learning

National Governors Association Center for Best Practices, Council of Chief State School Officers. (2010). Common Core State Standards. Washington, DC: Authors.

New York University. (2007) *National Symposium on the Millennial Student.* Retrieved from http://www.nyu.edu/frn/publications/millennial.student/Millennial.index.html

Partnership for 21st Century Skills. (2004). *The partnership for 21st century skills– Framework for 21st century learning.* Retrieved from http://www.p21.org/about-us/p21-framework

Sammons, L. (2009). *Guided math: a framework for mathematics instruction.* Huntington Beach: Shell Education.

Sammons, L. (2011, September 21). *Guided math: a framework for math instruction.* Retrieved June 25, 2015, from http://www.slideshare.net/ggierhart/guided-math-powerpointbytheauthorofguidedmath

Strategic Learning Programs. (n.d.). Retrieved from http://www.iste.org/lead/professional-services/strategic-learning-programs

Swanson, K. (2013, October 1). Tips for explaining common core to parents—*THE Journal.* Retrieved from http://thejournal.com/2013/10/01/how-to-explain-common-core-to-parents.aspx

Szybinski, D. (2007). From the Executive Director - *NETWORK: A Journal of Faculty Development.* Retrieved from http://tinyurl.com/pqwr7va

United States Congress. (2010) Section 1015c. Chapter 28: Higher education resources and student assistance. In *Title 20–Education* (2010 ed.). Retrieved from http://www.gpo.gov/fdsys/pkg/USCODE-2010-title20/html/USCODE-2010-title20-chap28.htm

DATE DUE